AF255504

SPEAK YOUR WAY TO SALES

Expert Strategies to Turn Speaking Into Sales, Clients, and Growth

Meredith Eaton | Jen Dalton |
Nancy D. Greene, Esq | Tracy Walker |
Molly Ruland | Heather McElrath |
Karlyn Ankrom | Jennifer Crawford |
Mary Sue Dahill | Katie Nelson

Published and distributed by Eaton Press, LLC

ISBN: 978-1-947486-29-4 (Hardcover)
ISBN: 978-1-947486-30-0 (Paperback)
ISBN: 978-1-947486-31-7 (Ebook)

TABLE OF CONTENTS

Collaboration among women is never accidental. It's strategic, generous, and powerful.

~ Meredith Eaton and Mary Sue Dahill

PREFACE

THE SPARK

The genesis of this collaborative book idea came from one of my former nonfiction writing clients, Mary Sue Dahill, with whom I worked to publish two books on technology and marketing for small businesses. Mary Sue proposed in 2022 that we initiate a project like this, but it wasn't the right time for me. I had just purchased a second virtual assistant business with my business partner, Jennifer Crawford, and was devoting 100 percent of my time to getting that company operationally healthy. However, when Mary Sue brought up the idea again in April 2025, I said yes.

THE JOURNEY

Mary Sue and I both know that being an author automatically confers expertise and that many small business owners, who are experts in their field, simply don't have the bandwidth to write an entire book. Our shared passion for writing and helping other small business owners elevate their message led us to launch a collaborative book project.

We wanted to develop this book differently from other nonfiction anthologies. Our goal was to ensure the book was inspirational, educational, and actionable around a single topic. With those goals and boundaries in mind, we quickly landed on the topic of speaking for lead generation because we know from experience that it is harder than it looks. From there, we began assembling a group of subject matter experts to build a strong lead-generation system for speaking opportunities. And I am not exaggerating when I say I learned at least one new thing from every single chapter.

What is a Collaborative Book?

Think of it as a smarter, more intentional evolution of the traditional nonfiction anthology. Instead of loosely connected essays, a collaborative book brings together carefully selected subject-matter experts to explore one focused topic, creating a cohesive, high-value masterclass for the reader.

Authors are chosen through an application process that ensures a strong mix of expertise and perspectives. Each chapter undergoes a developmental edit to align structure and style, resolve conflicting information, and highlight actionable tips. The result is a book that reads as if it were created by a unified team—because it is.

We created this model to avoid the common pitfalls of nonfiction anthologies, where themes can feel overly broad or disconnected. A collaborative book should be tight, relevant, and genuinely useful—not just a collection of unrelated chapters bound together.

To support that vision, we offer workshops, co-writing sessions, and marketing guidance throughout the project. Each author receives promotional materials, including a personalized book-cover graphic featuring their name, so they can confidently promote both their chapter and the full book.

Most importantly, this process doesn't just produce a polished book; it builds a community. Each project connects professionals who might not have met otherwise, creating lasting relationships that continue long after publication. As we expand into future collaborative books, we look forward to growing this network and the impact it creates.

Acknowledgements

This book would not be possible without the enthusiasm of Katie Nelson. Katie was immediately on board with a "Hell, yes!" as an author. She also helped shape how we presented this project to the authors.

Of course, this book would not be possible without the professional and beautiful collaboration of all our authors. Mary Sue and I were delighted by how smoothly this book went. All the authors were engaged, on time with deliverables, and thoughtful throughout the process.

I hope you will be as inspired by the ideas inside this book as I was and that you take the pieces that fit your style, experiment with the tools, and let each chapter nudge you toward a stronger, more strategic presence on and off the stage.

~ Meredith Eaton, Eaton Press
Developmental editor for *Speak Your Way to Sales*

Want the credibility of a book without writing the whole thing?

Scan the QR code to download **10x Your Business with a Collaborative Book** and see how one powerful chapter can boost your visibility, authority, and opportunities.

Start your author journey in the easiest way possible.

Scan to begin.

Introduction
by Meredith Eaton

Core Promise of the Book

Speak Your Way to Sales is for anyone who uses speaking to generate leads but struggles to turn those opportunities into real results. It is also for anyone who isn't using speaking to generate leads but wants to get started. My colleague and collaborative book partner, Mary Sue Dahill, and I have both used speaking to generate leads and clients for our businesses. We're both lucky to be "systems people"—the kind who love building and refining processes—so creating a speaking strategy that actually worked felt natural for us, not overwhelming. But as we talked with other business owners, it became clear that most lacked a solid speaking strategy, systems to stay organized, or a plan for what to do after the gig. That was when we knew that this would be the focus of our first collaborative book.

Why Strategy Matters

Most business professionals who speak invest a lot of time creating a great talk and finding opportunities to deliver it, but put little to no effort into the rest of the strategy. Creating a great presentation and finding people to listen to it are key parts of a speaking strategy, but they are not the entire strategy. And without a fully developed speaking strategy, it's nearly impossible to achieve the kind of outcomes that justify the effort of even creating the talk in the first place.

A fractured or undeveloped speaking strategy generally looks like:

- Speaking to audiences that don't completely align with you
- Lacking a system for post-event follow-up, which leaves money on the table
- Scattered and inefficient outreach that delivers a low ROI on effort
- Missed opportunities for leveraging your speaking gigs for social media content, other lead-generating activities, or finding more speaking opportunities
- Event planners love you, but don't rebook you because you aren't a good promotional partner

We could keep going, but the point is that if you're serious about using speaking as a business growth strategy, then it requires a fully developed plan that starts with finding gigs and ends with follow-up. It can become a self-propelling cycle, but *only* if it's built with that intention, and held up by solid systems.

That sounds like a lot, doesn't it? Don't get overwhelmed because *Speak Your Way to Sales* will give you everything you need to get started.

Our Promise to the Reader

With these challenges in mind, we have assembled a diverse group of experts who each provide inspiration, strategies, and action steps around each aspect of building a speaking strategy that yields results. We promise that after reading this book, you will have a roadmap for building your perfect speaker lead-generation system.

Without a robust system, you are asking too much from your talk and stage time. You must have additional support systems in place to truly make the most of your time on the stage.

What You Will Find Inside

We have organized the book into three parts that we hope will help lead you through what's needed for a repeatable, revenue-generating speaking system.

We open the book with three chapters to help speakers refine what they say and how they show up. Think of it as how to really own the mic because you have a rock-solid message and presence.

We begin with **Jen Dalton's chapter on the power of storytelling in building and communicating your brand.** A great speaker doesn't position themselves as the hero; they make the *audience* the hero of the story. Her chapter walks you through how to engage your audience before, during, and after an event so your message resonates long after you've stepped off stage. But Jen also makes it clear that branding is more than a logo. The real magic happens when you deeply understand your audience, intentionally design your brand experience, and develop stories—or talks—that attract the right people to your events. Her insights help speakers craft conversations that connect, convert, and create lasting brand loyalty.

Next, we have **Nancy Greene, who gets right to the heart of why we speak in the first place: impact.** But impact is only possible when your topic is relatable, not steeped in industry jargon or complicated concepts. As she says, "It does you no good to be the world's best bladdie-blah if no one benefits from your wisdom." The stories we tell as speakers should be mirrors for our audience, helping people see themselves, their challenges, and their solutions more clearly. Nancy's point is unforgettable: expertise only matters when it can be truly received.

Tracy Walker opens with the reminder that "confused people don't buy," and she shows you exactly what to do about it. Tracy's guide to increasing conversions with a powerful website begins your journey into the power of a good system. By making your website work as hard as you do, Tracy reframes marketing funnels as something far more human than a series of automated steps. In her words, your funnel isn't about being pushy; it's your gentle encore invitation, the way you whisper, "I see you; I value you," long after the mic is put away. She also introduces the power of repurposing your content (a theme that Karlyn Ankrom will expand on in her chapter). Tracy provides the foundational structure you will need to magnify the impact of speaking without multiplying your effort.

The next four chapters show how to create buzz, build trust, and become the kind of speaker event planners return to again and again. You want to be the speaker the audience remembers, and that comes from visibility, connection, and demand.

Podcast queen Molly Ruland brings a refreshing challenge to the way many speakers think about visibility: "Somewhere along the way, we quietly swapped connection for reach." Her chapter dives into the power of podcasts, not as a vanity metric but as a relationship engine. She teaches you to treat every podcast appearance as stepping into someone else's digital house and to be the kind of guest who gets invited back. It's not about chasing audience size or download numbers; it's about pursuing the right rooms, the right hosts, and the right listeners. As she reminds us, a podcast might have one hundred listeners, but if one of them is the right connector, collaborator, or champion, you may have just made your quarter. Relationships build leverage because trust travels faster than marketing does. I met my business partner (and *Speak Your Way to Sales* author) **Jennifer Crawford** through a relationship much like the ones Molly describes—proving her point that when you spend your time with people who energize you, everything in your business becomes more creative, more generous, and more magnetic.

Then Heather McElrath provides a masterclass in modern PR for speakers. Every inch of her chapter is packed with insight, actionable guidance, and strategic clarity for elevating your visibility. After laying the foundations of effective PR, her section on "quick PR wins for speakers" provides step-by-step instructions for generating media coverage and building credibility quickly. It's the kind of chapter you'll revisit again and again—part lesson, part checklist, and part accelerant for speakers ready to be seen.

The only way to follow Heather's PR class was through **Karlyn Ankrom's piece, in which she argues that your talk is far more than a single moment; it's a *content factory* with the power to keep you visible for months.** Every keynote, breakout session, or podcast guest appearance becomes raw material for social posts, videos, articles, lead magnets, and the ongoing conversations that build brand awareness "in the in-betweens" of your major speaking moments. Her chapter is a permission slip to stop letting your brilliance disappear once the applause dies down. Instead, she teaches you how to turn every stage appearance into a visibility machine. Karlyn teaches that repurposing isn't about reheating leftovers; it's about context-shifting. The core idea stays the same, but the frame changes so your message meets people exactly where they are, in the format they prefer.

Jennifer Crawford continues that theme by showing how relationship building is the goal behind the goal. Building a reputation as a sought-after speaker goes far beyond showing up with a polished talk. It's about being a dependable partner—meeting deadlines, creating compelling collateral, and staying engaged during and after an event. Jennifer's emphasis on using a virtual assistant to manage the workflows and systems complements Mary Sue's approach to pipeline management. Together, their chapters create a blueprint not only for creating opportunities but also for stewarding those opportunities with professionalism and consistency.

We conclude with our last two chapters on the systems that keep you booked and truly make speaking pay by turning speaking from a passion into a reliable revenue engine.

Mary Sue shows you how to turn interest into booked speaking gigs using a strategic CRM pipeline built for consistent outreach and follow-through. Instead of relying on luck or scattered notes, she gives you a simple system that keeps your opportunities moving and your follow-up tight. She makes a key distinction most speakers miss: outreach is the first ask, follow-up is how you stay on the radar once an event planner shows interest. A spreadsheet can store names, but it can't send reminders, track conversations, automate next steps, or manage agreements. A CRM pipeline does all of that, transforming scattered efforts into a steady flow of speaking opportunities and giving you the clarity to see what's working so you can land more gigs with confidence.

We close out this collection with **Katie Nelson's chapter, which argues that speaking isn't just a marketing activity; it *can be a revenue stream in its own right.*** Katie delivers the mindset, strategy, and system needed to turn speaking into a repeatable engine for revenue, one you can use to expand your business both now and in the future. She breaks it down into ten easy-to-remember steps, each designed to be applied at your current stage of business. Katie's message is simple and empowering: take what you need, implement it intentionally, and let every step bring in revenue. Speaking can—and should—pay off at every stage of the journey.

How to Get the Most out of This Book

I expect that every reader will need something different from this book, and every reader will get something they didn't know they needed as well. We have organized the chapters in a way that, to us, felt like it went from start to finish of a typical business development strategy. And that may be how this book works best for you as well. Or you may already have good systems in place but no strategies around PR or follow-up, so you may decide to go straight to those chapters.

We envision this as the type of book you may read through once and then reference repeatedly as your process or business evolves.

However you use this book, do not sleep on the additional content that each author provides. Use the QR codes to get additional tips and information and learn more about the authors and their services. If you need more support to set up your ideal speaking system, reach out to any of these authors to see what additional services they may offer that could change the game for you.

Pass the Mic to You

Beyond creating a strategic, inspirational, and actionable book, these authors also became a wonderful professional community. There has been networking within the author group; we have tapped some of the authors to work with us on marketing this and future books, and I know this is just the beginning of how I will be enriched, personally and professionally, for having undertaken this collaborative book project.

On behalf of Mary Sue and me, we hope that you find this book as helpful and inspirational as we do and that you go forth and build an amazing custom speaking strategy that will transform your business.

Meredith Eaton

Ceo, Eaton Press, LLC
Co-CEO, Sparent, LLC
Co-CEO, Move Forward Virtual
Assistants, LLC

EatonPress.com
sparent.co
moveforwardvirtualassistants.com
@sparentco
@moveforwardvas

Meredith Eaton is the CEO of Eaton Press, where she has spent over a decade helping business professionals turn their expertise into powerful nonfiction books. With a proven track record of guiding authors to write books that open doors to speaking engagements and fuel business growth, Meredith is passionate about transforming ideas into impact. Through her signature programs and personalized support, she empowers entrepreneurs to become published authorities in their fields.

In *Speak Your Way to Sales*, Meredith opens the book with an insightful introduction and lead the developmental editing process, ensuring every chapter reflects the author's unique voice and expertise.

Meredith is also the Co-CEO of Sparent, LLC, and Move Forward Virtual Assistants, serving businesses and mental health practices.

Beyond being a CEO, Meredith enjoys spending time with her 4 grandchildren, going to the beach as often as possible, and doing jigsaw puzzles while watching reality TV or crime shows.

Education, Certifications, & Accreditations

- Received an M.A. in Organizational Management from George Washington University
- Earned a certificate in The Psychology of Leadership from Cornell University
- Serves as a mentor for undergrad entreprenuership students

1

CRAFTING YOUR PERSONAL BRAND STORY FOR THE STAGE
BY JEN DALTON

*"Storytelling is the most powerful way
to put ideas into the world today."*
—Robert McKee

Storytelling is a critical part of communicating your brand because it creates a connection with the audience. Telling a story makes it easier for your audience to relate to you and your topic, recall the story later, and share it with others. According to the Stanford Graduate School of Business, stories are remembered up to twenty-two times more than facts alone. (Aaker, n.d.) When it comes to defining one's personal brand and company brand, strong storytelling crafts the heart and the why of a brand. When a business owner, entrepreneur, leader, or speaker utilizes storytelling, they drive higher conversion rates and brand loyalty while connecting intentionally with their ideal customer (and audience). Therefore, as individuals think about building their brand, understanding the story of their business and their why increases their relatability to their ideal audience, which is paramount.

Building a Personal Brand for the Stage

A powerhouse personal brand we all recognize would be Taylor Swift. Readers may roll their eyes or totally agree when reading that last sentence. Taylor Swift has built a global following by inviting the audience to participate in her story and brand. Her followers experience narrative immersion, becoming brand advocates and champions. The reality is that Taylor Swift utilizes storytelling in a powerful way. Her audience finds themselves inside her stories, whether it's because they relate to her songs, are invited to secret launch parties, or are hunting for the latest "easter egg." Master storytellers make the audience the hero and main character in their stories.

It is helpful for speakers to consider the entire experience, from before a talk to during a talk, and after a talk. What story or experience is being created, and how can the speaker help their audience join in? Sometimes, it can be as simple as providing a video beforehand, inviting them to be ready. It can include providing materials for them to engage with during the talk. Afterwards, it can be follow-up outreach via different channels to maintain connection.

A Business Brand Can Play a Role in the Story Too

Not all speakers require both a personal brand and a business brand. However, there is a role for a business brand to play in expanding the foundation and potential scalability of a person's impact. One of my favorite brands is Patagonia. Their logo is a silhouette of Mount Fitz Roy, a dramatic peak that straddles the border between Chile and Argentina. The logo tells the story of the brand's commitment to respecting nature, perseverance, and exploration. The font is clear and crisp, highlighting trust and transparency. Beyond the logo, the heart of Patagonia's brand is its mission: to build the best products while causing no unnecessary harm and to use business to protect nature. Patagonia lives its values of quality and customer care day to day. Its brand is consistent, like a heartbeat. The brand is authentic, purpose-driven, and invests in real action aligned with its mission, while creating high-quality products.

One of the best examples of how Patagonia leveraged storytelling was when it invited its audience to be "heroes" in the Patagonia Worn Wear program. In 2013, Patagonia launched this program to help customers keep their outdoor apparel in use for as long as possible by repairing, trading in, or caring for items rather than replacing them. The program expanded with dedicated repair tours and facilities, offering both mail-in and in-store services, as well as DIY repair resources and free patch kits. Patagonia was actively living their brand values, focused on sustainability, not sales.

When speaking from the stage, successful business owners make their audience the hero of the story and intentionally engage them before, during, and after an event. Crafting a logo is just the beginning. Understanding your audience, designing a brand, and developing relevant stories (talks) to attract people to your events is where the magic happens.

In this chapter, readers will learn how to move from a visual identity to delivering an audience-centric story that gives their brand a heartbeat and increases engagement.

Crafting Your Origin Story

Whether capturing an origin story for a business or a talk, the process is the same. A person notices something that is broken or not working through their experiences or observations. After validating the story through informal conversations, focus groups, or research, a person builds a story that communicates the challenge and a potential solution to the problem. The solution could be a service or product-based business, talks, social media content, writing, and more. To be relevant, we must raise awareness of the problem and the solution, utilizing a storytelling approach.

WHAT PROBLEM DO YOU SEE?

When I launched BrandMirror, I did so because I saw that too many people were unhappy in their work and lives. I believed that if people knew their value and purpose, they could increase their odds of success and find fulfillment and meaning. This drove my focus on creating processes, approaches, and talks to help individuals find their why, identify their unique value, and communicate it in ways that increase their visibility, impact, and opportunities. Since then, I have delivered hundreds of talks to nonprofits, businesses, government agencies, and more.

Here are amazing examples of thought leaders who created an impact through storytelling from the stage. Keep in mind, they started by taking a first step at some point, too. These are the top TED talks that all started as ideas born of experience.

- Brené Brown: The Power of Vulnerability
- Simon Sinek: How Great Leaders Inspire Action
- Sir Ken Robinson: Do Schools Kill Creativity?
- Tim Urban: Inside the Mind of a Master Procrastinator
- Amy Cuddy: Your Body Language May Shape Who You Are

These amazing speakers spent years being curious and seeking to understand a fundamental challenge they observed in the world. They also developed mental frameworks and models to explain their topics.

FROM PURPOSE TO PERSONAL BRAND

Each individual and organization should have an origin story and clearly articulate their why, what they excel at, and how they deliver value.

- Define your purpose and why.
- Define what you do.
- Describe how you do it.

Once you articulate these three things, the next step is to align them with who your audiences might be and with the expertise you have or need to be credible. I think of expertise as topics on which people regularly seek my information. In addition, expertise includes what I am extremely knowledgeable about. It is relevant to think through what "bundles of knowledge" your personal and company brands bring to bear. A personal brand and a company brand may overlap; however, the founder's expertise and the business's expertise will most likely differ. From this perspective, we can package our expertise into content for keynotes, workshops, podcasts, panels, and more.

> *"Life isn't about finding yourself.*
> *Life is about creating yourself."*
> **—George Bernard Shaw**

How to Begin Crafting Your Personal Story for the Stage

Begin by identifying one to three topics you have a deep passion for and expertise in that you believe are essential for people to know. These topics could cover hard skills, soft skills, or both. For example, if you come from the AI industry and want to start a business focused on implementing AI effectively, that would be the key topic area to include in your speaking toolkit. If you have experience coaching new hires and existing team members on utilizing AI, this would be another area of expertise to reference. From these areas of expertise, you would create topics for talks like: "Ethics in AI," "How to Scale Your Team's AI Skills," or "How to Lead Through the AI Transformation."

Craft Your Reputation Rings

One helpful exercise to identify potential topics is to draw a Venn diagram with three circles. In each circle, write down an area of expertise that you have. Here is an example of my Reputation Rings (aka Venn diagram) and the "bundles of knowledge" I could speak to at a high level. I share this visual to show how to construct your Venn diagram and what brainstorming your bundles of knowledge might look like. What is important to note is that some bundles of knowledge exist in only one circle, while others overlap two or three circles. When it comes to standing out, it is important to reflect on your expertise and craft a message or a talk that sets you apart. Where more than one skill overlaps with others is where the magic and creativity of talk ideas can happen. Even if others have given similar talks, your message may resonate differently with an audience. Your story matters.

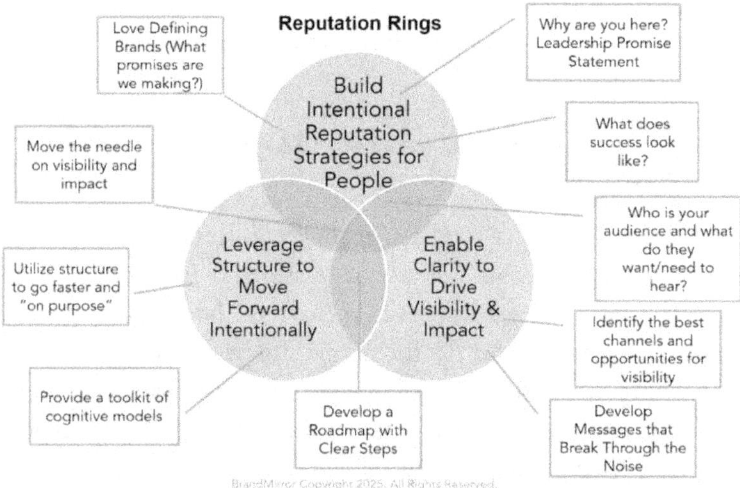

UTILIZE YOUR EXPERIENCES

Another way to brainstorm talk ideas is to write down pivotal events in your career and life, and what you learned from them. Our personal brand will likely include expertise outside of our jobs, too. It could include volunteer work, service, education, sports, family, networking, etc. Speaking and storytelling from the stage requires sharing material that informs, inspires, ignites, and influences the audience. I call this the Four Is that are not about you. Who needs to know what you know? Identify three to five audiences who would be interested in hearing about a topic you could deliver. Before writing the talk or creating materials, write down the topic and a brief description of what you would cover and what the audience's takeaways would be. It is important to utilize storytelling and include some data; however, do not overwhelm the audience. Often, data can be a great hook if you share a surprising statistic. A great hook can also be a personal story that grabs the audience.

> *"Stories are just data with a soul."*
> *—Brené Brown, TEDx Houston 2010*

Be Humble and Curious

A next step would be to Google or ask an AI for similar talk titles and descriptions, who delivered it, and where it was held. Your talk doesn't need to be the only one of its kind ever. The reality is that others have spoken about 99 percent of the same material you may cover. However, 100 percent of other talks will never be like your talk because you have unique experiences and insights. Just like one would research a business or company idea, it is helpful to analyze what content (talks, podcasts, panels, blogs, videos, etc.) already exists. Research may uncover ideas for tweaking a talk and where it could be delivered, as well as new ways to consider delivering it.

Ideas and Content Can Kickstart Storytelling

If you have written a blog or a book, for example, most of the content can be converted into a talk, or vice versa. I had an experience where I was discussing politics with my husband, and we began arguing. That experience led me to research difficult conversations, which led to a TEDx talk audition a few months later and, nine months later, to my book, *Listen.* A story that connects with the audience should be relatable, genuine, and insightful. At the end of the day, it is the conversation we want to join, shape, or start that drives what talks we design and develop.

> ***"You want to build your brand before you need it."***
> **—Jen Dalton**

BUILDING A PERSONAL BRAND FOR SPEAKING

The key to building a brand is to do so consistently. When developing a talk, consider writing about the topic on social media and begin implementing a "bread crumb strategy" to show your audience that you have a perspective on the topic. Then, as you build your visibility and expertise bit by bit, when you announce a talk, it will be received as a matter of course. Sometimes people announce they are speaking on a topic without evidence of expertise, which can be jarring and, at best, create cognitive dissonance and, at worst, break trust or believability. For example, a credibility ladder spread out over several months could look like this (illustrative only):

Step 1: Social media posts on a topic
Step 2: Write one or more blogs
Step 3: Create a video about the topic
Step 4: Write a newsletter (LinkedIn, for example)
Step 5: Deliver your own webinar or in-person talk
Step 6: Create or join a panel discussion on your topic
Step 7: Be on a podcast
Step 8: Deliver a workshop
Step 9: Deliver a talk
Step 10: Deliver a keynote

You are on your way!

It is important to identify what you can do and set expectations around that. Typically, building your brand as a speaker can take at least six months to twelve months or more. In addition to building your voice and credibility, the next step is to build your evidence.

Show Me the Speaker! Errr, Money!

First impressions matter, and your personal brand should be well defined and presented in a compelling way. At a minimum, build up to three talks in your toolkit. Once you have delivered a few talks, the next step would be to create a speaker one-pager. This should include your headshot, name, high-level key phrases, places where you have given talks, a short speaker bio, a short description of your talks, testimonials, social media, etc. Visit https://brandmirror.com/talks-workshops/ to download my speaker kit for ideas.

An intentional next step would be to add "Speaker" to your LinkedIn profile, both in the headline and as an "Experience" entry. Updating your bio, social profiles, website, and more are all part of presenting a cohesive personal brand as a trusted speaker. When moving from a free or stipend speaker to higher speaker fees, this evidence goes a long way toward showing your value. In addition, when there is an opportunity, create a "sizzle reel" or "speaker reel" that showcases snippets from your talks in a compelling way. One way to create a sizzle reel is to pull from videos, podcast recordings, or other shorter talks to attract larger audiences.

Stick to Your Story

As a speaker, you may be asked to expand what you talk about for a prospect or client. Be mindful that staying in your lane as much as possible is important. It is okay to tailor a talk to an audience, event, or business; however, be sure you can deliver a great experience. Earlier, I shared the Venn diagram tool; this is a great way to ensure you hold yourself accountable for the talks and content you promise to deliver.

Do I Need More Than a Personal Brand as a Speaker?

There are cases where people build their personal brand to speak for an organization, a business, or just on their own, out of passion. As part of your personal brand, be clear on your personality, energy, rhythm, and how you make your audience feel. Often, speakers are referred to because of their personal brand, and it is the individual who is spoken about to others. Some speakers launch their own personal social channels, website, merchandise, signature "personalized" logo, and more. Here are a few examples of personal brands that have become business brands. Several of them also have a business brand, though their name tends to outshine it.

- David Rubenstein
- Mel Robbins
- Oprah
- Seth Godin
- Gary Vee

There are, however, times when having a business brand can boost your personal brand's visibility, credibility, and relevance.

How to Craft and Utilize a Business Brand for the Stage

As an entrepreneur, business owner, or executive, there is a strategic role for the business brand as a launch pad for speaking engagements. A business brand may be more relevant at different events and can open doors that a personal brand may need help opening. A business brand can provide awareness, authority, and access for a speaker at any level. I have worked with many clients who began speaking at events representing their companies and leveraged those appearances to help them launch their personal brands.

Crafting or Understanding the Business Brand

Like capturing your personal brand, a business brand should also go through a Reputation Rings exercise. It is helpful to identify the three areas in which a business excels and where they overlap. The different areas can inform what expertise a business has, what leaders might speak about, where they might speak, and what kinds of talks will be used. A business brand can add additional legitimacy when seeking speaking opportunities.

Expand Your Topics

As a leader or executive at a company, this can provide a unique opportunity to speak about culture, leadership, mentorship, or digital transformation—whatever your company excels at or has experienced and navigated. Some of these talks will require employees; however, many are relevant to a solopreneur as well. From partnerships to growing pains, a solopreneur has experiences they can share in a powerful way, building their personal and business brand at the same time.

Visibility at Industry Functions

A business brand, especially a larger one, can elevate speakers for panels, keynotes, workshops, and more through brand association and potentially a high level of trust in the brand. Another way a business brand can lend gravitas is by sponsoring an event. This can be pay-to-play, which turns some people off. However, depending on your business and marketing strategy, that might be the right choice. For a new speaker, leveraging the business's brand can be an excellent way to accelerate becoming known as a storyteller and expert in your field.

Consider Nonprofit and Board Service

When it comes to speaking, do not underestimate the opportunity to build a brand as a speaker while serving on nonprofit boards or boards in general. Whether it is speaking internally at a Town Hall or a gala, there is room to build and practice your speaking skills intentionally. Recently, I created a webinar with the Business

Women's Giving Circle in Northern Virginia to feature four women who had served on various boards. Not only did this event provide value to listeners, but it also gave each speaker a chance to add to their thought leadership expertise.

CREATE THE OPPORTUNITY FOR STORYTELLING

Sometimes, when using a business brand for speaking, we forget to address other areas like leadership, community service, board work, etc. As a board member or even a volunteer, consider what a panel, podcast, mini-workshop, or conference might look like in terms of helping others and boosting your brand's visibility. Often, people are waiting to be discovered as a speaker, when in reality this requires jumping in and going for it intentionally.

As leaders and organizations, the ability to paint a new, engaging picture that helps your audience know what to do next is a critical skill. A powerful story meets your audience where they are, connects emotionally by being relatable, and inspires them to take action with a compelling vision of the future.

> ***"Stories create the emotional context people need to locate themselves in a larger experience."***
> ***—Scott Bedbury***

WHEN TO USE PERSONAL VS. BUSINESS BRANDING FOR SPEAKING

For company-led events, a business brand can position an individual as an industry spokesperson and open larger stages. For expert-led events or audiences seeking authentic connection, a personal brand creates resonance, relatability, and expanded opportunities across multiple industries. Ideally, both should work together. The personal brand attracts attention, and the business brand amplifies authority and reach. When it comes to increasing your speaking fees, it is important to remember that they are directly determined by your likability, relevance, expertise, and perceived value to an organization.

Many speakers have launched their personal brands through innovative work they have done for an organization. The business brand provides a platform for a person to share more than one story, expanding reach and giving the brand a face. You can explore a few highlights from the BigSpeak website here: https://www.bigspeak.com/.

- Guy Kawasaki is a top innovation keynote speaker, social media expert, chief evangelist of Canva, and a bestselling author. His entertaining, informative talks draw on insights from his time in the tech industry to show audiences how to create innovative services and products using tactical, practical techniques.

- Jocko Willink is a retired U.S. Navy SEAL who now works as a leadership instructor, strategic advisor, speaker, and podcaster. He has successfully translated his over two-decade experience as a SEAL team leader into developing business managers into formidable leaders. His approach is one of *Extreme Ownership*, the same name for his #1 New York Times bestselling book.

Building a Brand with Heart and a Story to Tell

We should love our personal and business brands. If you do not love your brand yet, continue practicing and updating your story library. Should you need to pivot in your life and career, speaking and storytelling can go a long way to help you move forward. Creating brands allows us to craft our stories with intention. As we tell stories, remember the goal is to understand what we want our audience to know, feel, and do.

Storytelling is far more than a creative skill. It's a foundational strategy for both personal and business branding. As Robert McKee famously notes, the power of story lies in its ability to breathe life into ideas and foster genuine connection. The most enduring brands and memorable leaders don't simply present facts or features; they weave narratives that invite audiences to see themselves in the story, building empathy, trust, and community along the way. Whether you're defining the origins of your brand, sharing your expertise, or taking the stage to inspire action, story infuses your message with authenticity and relevance. Ultimately, effective storytelling bridges purpose and engagement, transforming abstract ideas into movements that stick and spread and anchoring your brand in the hearts and minds of those you seek to reach.

"I believe people should be able to do something differently the moment they leave the room. I consider a great talk one that is thought-provoking and has actionable insights."

—Jen Dalton, Founder, BrandMirror

* * *

References

Aaker, Jennifer. n.d. "Harnessing the Power of Stories | VMware Women's Leadership Innovation Lab." VMware Women's Leadership Innovation Lab. Accessed September 30, 2025. https://womensleadership.stanford.edu/resources/voice-influence/harnessing-power-stories.

Smith, Anna K. 2023. "Here is Why You have Every Right to be Unhappy at Work." Here is Why You have Every Right to be Unhappy at Work. https://www.forbes.com/sites/annkowalsmith/2023/12/15/heres-why-you-have-every-right-to-be-unhappy-at-work/.

Ready to amplify your brand and impact?

Schedule a free consult with Jen Dalton today to clarify your unique value and accelerate your visibility.

Scan the QR Code to access:

- ☑ Connect on LinkedIn
- ☑ Schedule a Consult
- ☑ Download Your LinkedIn Checklist
- ☑ Download Your Personal Brand Worksheet
- ☑ and even more!!!

Telepathy is not a strategy.
Contact Jen directly at
jendalton@brandmirror.com or call 703-898-8691
for bookings, questions, or inquiries.

Jen Dalton

BrandMirror

www.brandmirror.com

linkedin.com/in/jennifervdalton

@jenvdalton

Jen Dalton is the CEO and founder of BrandMirror, where she specializes in personal branding strategy, working with executives, entrepreneurs, and organizations to clarify their purpose, elevate their visibility, and create lasting impact in their industries.

With over 20 years of experience in brand and business strategy, Jen has partnered with Fortune 500 companies, coached thousands of leaders, published bestselling books such as *The Intentional Entrepreneur* and *Listen*, and been recognized as an Entrepreneurial Leader of the Year at Georgetown University. She is an international speaker, author, and certified personal brand strategist who helps leaders and organizations define, deliver, and amplify their unique value and promise.

In *Speak Your Way to Sales*, Jen shares actionable strategies for leveraging your personal brand to build confidence, shape your narrative, and spark meaningful conversations that drive results. This ties the chapter's focus back to helping professionals authentically connect and convert through intentional talks and speaking engagements.

Beyond her professional focus, Jen enjoys giving back to the community through board service at organizations helping families and women leaders, living in Northern Virginia with her family, and pursuing passion projects in leadership development and storytelling.

Education, Certifications, & Accreditations

- EMBA, Georgetown University McDonough School of Business (2010–2012)
- BSBA, International Management & Human Resources, Georgetown University (1995–1999)
- Master Personal Brand Strategist & 360 Reach Analyst, Reach Personal Branding
- PROSCI Change Management Certification
- 1 Million Cups Certified Organizer (Kauffman Foundation)
- Strategies that Build Winning Brands, Kellogg School of Management (Northwestern University)

2

SPEAKING IN STORIES:
TURNING COMPLEX TOPICS
INTO RELATABLE IDEAS
BY NANCY D. GREENE, ESQ.

I'm not your typical lawyer. You're more likely to see a full-size Dalek and movie memorabilia in my office than a law degree on my wall. When asked to describe myself, I'll tell you I'm a Sci-Fi fantasy geek, writer, and lawyer. See what got the top billing there? Don't get me wrong. I love being a lawyer. I just tend to look at things a bit differently than your standard business law and litigation attorney. Add into the mix that I started practicing law when women were still expected to wear skirts to court, and yup, I have a very different perspective than a lot of my peers. It's one of the reasons I became a speaker: I needed to talk to women business owners and entrepreneurs about the steps they needed to take, but rarely did, to protect their businesses.

I'd been a lawyer for fifteen years and a solo practitioner for three years, and I noticed a lot of my clients were facing the same issue. They'd gone into business with their husband's friend, racquetball partner, or someone he knew from church. The male business partner usually had the experience or the startup capital. They would go into business without any corporate documents in place because they were friends, and they would work it out. After all, a handshake is just as good as a contract. Well, isn't it? We know what we intend.

The business became successful, meaning it was making more money than it cost to run, and then the problems started. That's one of the secrets they don't tell you when you start a business with someone else: the good times are just as likely to cause problems as the bad. There would be a dispute about how to operate the business or who should be paid what. At the end of the day, the women business owner ended up on the losing side. She lost her time, investment, her stake in the company, and her self-confidence—all because she trusted when she should have documented. It's not just "trust but verify;" it's "trust and create a paper trail."

Now, you would think people would flock to talks that help them have better relationships with their business partners, collect their client accounts, and manage their employees.

Yeah.

Not so much.

The reality is the law is scary. People would rather attend that sexy marketing session or learn how to use generative artificial intelligence in their business than learn how to leverage the law to ensure they have the proper foundation for their business. (I'm not bitter or anything.) So, what do you do when your topic is something that your audience absolutely needs but is absolutely something they do not want to focus on?

Well, you talk about Daleks, Cybermen, and Dr. Who.

Seriously.

A woman, on the verge of tears, came up to talk to me after one of my early speaking gigs. She had been afraid to get legal advice for her business because every attorney she had talked to had made her feel stupid because she didn't understand the law. She was so grateful my talk had answered her questions in a way she understood. We spent the next month ensuring her business had the proper contracts and documentation to thrive.

Those lawyers and speakers she'd gone to before me had missed a critical point—actually, the only point. It does you no good to be the world's best bladdie-blah if no one benefits from your wisdom. So, you have to break your topic down into something meaningful and relatable to your audience, but also authentic to who you are. I'll never (well, almost never) use a sports analogy because I'm not a huge sports fan and my chosen sport—competition show riding—is pretty niche. Instead, I will draw on examples from my cases, relate them to pop culture, and speak plainly because that's who I am. Not every one of my learned friends (that's lawyer speak for other lawyers) can be a speaker. Too many of them are trapped by thinking in legal jargon.

It takes skill to translate "lawyer" into "real person." It does no good for me to tell you we're going to apply the *res ipsa loquitor* doctrine if you have no idea what that means. (And you shouldn't; that's why you hired an attorney, after all.) It is equally unhelpful when you ask a lawyer what they mean, and they give you the literal translation of the Latin and tell you, "The thing speaks for itself." Eh? But if I told you it meant "that shit doesn't happen unless someone messed up, so we don't have to prove exactly *how* they messed up because the law assumes they did." Now you get the concept. It makes sense that the log coming off the truck to smash into that windshield in *Final Destination* was because someone forgot to tie down the load, and not because of some vast eldritch force, right?

Right?

Anyway…

The stories we tell as speakers are mirrors for our audience. They need to be able to see their reflections in both the successes and risks of the pitfalls. Starting a business is one of the most exciting and terrifying things a person can do. Because of this, they often rush off without stopping at "Go" and collecting their $200. But you can't build long-term success this way. We're great at deceiving ourselves that *this* horror story or *that* tale of woe will never happen to *me*. Our job as speakers is to help our audience see that the ugly reality is that those tales of woe can happen to anyone, and then to provide them with the building blocks of a solution.

As I said, the impetus for me to leave the comfy space of my desk and the courtroom and venture onto a stage was to educate more women on how to avoid falling victim to the same fact pattern I was seeing repeatedly.

The one that broke the proverbial camel's back? It actually combined two of the worst things I was seeing time and again: no documentation and no verification processes in place due to unwarranted trust.

My client, Jane, went into business with her husband's acquaintance, Harry, buying gold and jewelry. Harry had been in this line of business before and was supposed to teach Jane everything she needed to know. They were equal partners, although they had no corporate paperwork to that effect. The business, All About Gold ("AAG"), quickly became successful. Harry's son, Junior, took the scrap jewelry to the refinery for sale and then reported the sales price to Harry and Jane via text message. Junior received a check for part of the sales price and cash for the rest. Harry would then deposit the check and split the cash with Jane as their distribution.

However, it turned out that when Junior texted the sales, he was underreporting the cash he received from the refinery, which Harry then kept for himself. Harry felt entitled to the extra money because, of course, it was "really" his business, and Jane wouldn't have it without him. He also felt fairly safe doing so because it was cash; how would Jane find out? Eventually, Jane realized the company's revenue was dropping for no apparent reason. She started going to the refinery with her sales, rather than letting Junior take them. The refinery owner said some things that added to Jane's concerns.

Enter yours truly. A review of what little books Harry kept on his transactions showed more irregularities. We sued to kick him out of the company (disassociate a member from a limited liability company) for an accounting of his transactions and for fraud. Because we had a lawsuit in place, I was able to force the refinery to give me a copy of its records. While Harry and Junior didn't have any reason to keep accurate records, the refinery didn't have any reason to falsify their records. The refinery records showed the hundreds of thousands of dollars that had been stolen from the business. Once we reconstructed the business records, we settled the case and removed Harry and Junior from the business.

I tell this story from the stage to create interest in and context for a fairly boring legal topic: paperwork. It lays the groundwork for what I want to teach the audience about leveraging legal paperwork to better protect themselves. While, as a speaker, you might not have to guard yourself against a literal dishonest gold thief (instead, you'll be concerned about whether you can sell from the stage, if there's a revenue share agreement and access to attendee contact information), but you want to be sure your stories lead into your teaching points. The more your clients want to avoid your teaching points, the more interesting—and dramatic—your stories and presentations need to be.

Another dramatic example I love using in my presentations shows how negotiations about key contract terms with a potential business partner can reveal the potential for future problems. One of the provisions I like to include in the corporate documents I draft is one to remove "transgressing" members or shareholders, respectively. These provisions allow the other partners to remove a "bad actor" and devalue their interest in the business through the resulting buyback. Every single time, the people who have objected to these provisions have been those who, ultimately, my clients were better off not being in business with. Fahim wanted to bring a partner, Taahir, into his established business as a minority shareholder who would earn his stock based on certain financial benchmarks. But Taahir wanted to have all decisions made unanimously and objected to the Transgressing Shareholder clause. I explained to Fahim that by requiring unanimous consent for all decisions, Taahir, who would at most be a 10 percent shareholder, would effectively be exercising equal control over the company, rendering Fahim's majority interest meaningless. We also discussed the pros and cons of having a business owner who was worried about repercussions for his bad acts, such as competing against the company, and how that would impact the business. Ultimately, Fahim withdrew the offer of ownership and hired Taahir as an employee. Fast forward several years, and we ran into issues with Taahir when we learned he was diverting work from the company to a business he solely owned. He left the company screaming, "Exterminate!" (see, I told you I'd work Daleks in here somewhere) as he tried to steal the company's largest clients. Because he never became an "owner," he lacked access to certain information that could have devastated the company had he had access to it, and Fahim didn't have to sue to wrestle control of his company back from Taahir when he became a "bad actor." Fahim just fired him. Having tough discussions at the start of the relationship as part of documenting your business agreements and processes can save that business and your sanity down the road.

If you speak about a topic your ideal customer wants to avoid thinking about (a tough love topic), it's imperative that you present the topic in the most approachable way possible. People don't want to think about the business partner who steals from them or the employee who tries to take the clients with them when they leave. It helps to admit that the topic's just hard. There is usually a noticeable relaxation of postures in the room if not outright sighs of relief when I admit that even I struggle with things like employee/independent contractor or overtime classifications, and I do this for a living. Everyone likes to know they are not alone in the struggle.

Tough-love topics can be either really fun to speak on or the opposite. I always start with the fun. At the end of the talk, my audience feels confident that if they need to have a hard business conversation, I'm the right ally to have.

Speaking of struggle, how do you speak to an audience about managing someone's expectations? Whether you're speaking on marketing, coaching, hiring employees, client management systems, or any other product or service, at the end of the day, we all have to manage our audience's and clients' expectations. If we don't, even if we do our best work, whether it's a kick ass presentation or a plan for wiping out the Cybermen, it will disappoint.

How do you manage expectations?

Clearly set expectations.

What do I mean by this?

EXTERMINATE AMBIGUITY!

Oh, sorry. The Dalek took over the keyboard for a second. Anyway…

When we speak, we give our audience a roadmap for the journey we will take them on. We touch base and refer to points on the journey often, so they don't get lost. For the business side of our speaking operation, we need clear written contracts that refer to the benchmarks. If we don't, we risk misunderstandings, unhappy customers, and loss of our business. Dario ran a small bookkeeping business. Rather than incur the expenses related to a new business, Big Time Corp ("BTC") kept New Co's financial records as if it were a separate division within its own books. Later, BTC wanted to properly create New Co's financial records. BTC hired Dario to separate the companies' financial transactions and manage their QuickBooks accounts for the next year. They verbally agreed to a fee for the work and a monthly fee for the ongoing bookkeeping for both companies. Dario was particularly proud of the product he turned in. New Co had a brand-new set of records, and BTC's records had the New Co transactions labeled and set aside from its financial dealings. Unfortunately, BTC's CEO, Javier, was not happy. Javier expected that the New Co transactions would be deleted from BTC's records. Because Javier and Dario never discussed what the final product would look like, they each had different expectations, and no benchmarks were set to identify the differences before delivery of the end product. BTC refused to pay for the work and cancelled the services agreements. The dispute and Dario's loss of income could have been avoided if expectations had been discussed, managed, and documented. Setting expectations is critical.

The non-legal advice in my talks may be the most important parts, though. Always meet your audience and clients where they are. Never talk down to them. Remember, you are holding a mirror up to them, which means you'll be reflecting their fears, hopes, or dreams. Do so with compassion and humor and give them a path forward. I'll let the Doctor help me voice my final thoughts:

"We're all capable of the most incredible change. We can evolve while still staying true to who we are. We can honor who we've been and choose who we want to be next." —*The Thirteenth Doctor,* Season 11, Episode 1: "The Woman Who Fell to Earth" (2018)

After all, isn't this why we speak—to evolve and assist while honoring that incredible change in others?

Find out how to navigate Legal Landmines

Scan the QR Code to:

☑ Schedule a consultation
☑ Book Nancy as a speaker
☑ Watch videos explaining legal issues
☑ Find answers to legal questions

Nancy D. Greene, Esq.

N D Greene, PC

NGDLaw.com

linkedin.com/in/attorneynancygreene/

facebook.com/nancy.greene.595335

Nancy D. Greene is the CEO at N D Greene PC where she loves working with other women and helping them avoid legal landmines while navigate the very stormy waters of running a business in today's litigious society. Repeatedly introduced as "not your typical lawyer," Nancy demystifies legal "mumbo-jumbo."

With 30 of legal experience, Nancy has been a national speaker since 2014. She published *Navigating Legal Landmines* an Amazon Best Seller in 2017. She specializes in advising businesses about employment law, employee dishonesty issues, business law, mergers and acquisitions, shareholder agreements and disputes, ongoing operations, and bankruptcy.

In *Speak Your Way to Sales*, Nancy shares how to speak about tough issues on the stage and in your business.

Beyond the law, Nancy writes fiction and historical romance, enjoys riding and all things beach related. She lives on a horse farm with her husband and far too many animals (according to him).

Education, Certifications, & Accreditations

Juris Doctorate, Catholic University, Washington DC, 1995
Bar Associations, Virginia (1995); Maryland (1996), DC (1996)
Publisher/writer, *Navigating Legal Landmines, 2017*
YouTube Channel, www.youtube.com/@attorneynancygreene8669
Founder, N D Greene PC, January 2019

3

The Encore Effect:
Systems That Keep the
Conversation Going
by Tracy Walker

Beautiful speaker, this chapter is for you.

You already know the power of standing on stage, the way your words ignite hearts and plant seeds of change. You've dedicated yourself to delivering talks that spark both understanding and inspiration. And yet, if you're reading this, it's because you want more than applause.

You want the right people, the ones nodding, leaning in, and whispering, "Yes, this is what I've been waiting for," to become clients. You want the impact you spark on stage to echo long after the lights dim.

This isn't about hustling harder or chasing every lead. It's about creating systems that capture the magic of your moment and carry it forward.

Because here's the truth: more leads don't come from doing more; they come from harnessing the momentum you've already built.

So let this chapter be your encore. Think of it as your personal backstage crew, encouraging you, providing tools, and reminding you that your message matters and deserves the spotlight.

Take a deep breath. You don't have to figure it all out today. Just know this: *you already have what it takes.* Together, we'll ensure your talk doesn't just end with applause. It opens the door to meaningful connections and lasting impact.

Now let's do what you do best: shine on stage.

YOUR ENCORE OFFER: EXTENDING THE CONVERSATION

When you invite your audience to act in the moment, you're saying, "I want to keep walking with you." This is where inspiration becomes transformation and where applause ripples into long-term connection.

Think about it: when someone is sitting in your audience, they're fully present, emotionally connected, nodding in agreement. This is the sweet spot. If you wait until later, you risk losing the spark.

That's why your encore invitation matters. It's not just a call-to-action. It's a bridge between the energy of the stage and the next step in the relationship.

WHAT AN ENCORE INVITATION CAN LOOK LIKE

- **Text-to-Opt-In Codes:** Share a simple keyword your audience can text from their seats.
- **QR Codes:** Display a scannable code that links directly to your lead magnet or resource.
- **Live Polls or Surveys:** Engage them in real time while capturing insights.
- **Giveaways or Prizes:** A fun way to collect info and spark excitement.

WHY THIS WORKS

An encore invitation captures the momentum you've just created and keeps it alive. Think of it as the digital version of saying, "Don't just clap; come join me backstage." It extends the energy of the moment and turns excitement into action.

MAKE THE NEXT STEP EFFORTLESS

In my experience, the easiest steps are always the ones people actually take, and that's where real momentum begins. The truth is simple: if the next step feels hard, most people won't take it. When things are confusing, overwhelming, or time-consuming, attention drops fast.

However, when you make that next step easy—clear instructions, minimal clicks, no extra barriers—you send a strong message. You're showing people that you value their time, you respect their energy, and you want to help them win. And that's how you keep the excitement alive and moving forward.

AFTER THE APPLAUSE

The house lights dim. Your keynote's final words linger. You're greeted with hugs, handshakes, and eager conversations. And you know without question: you nailed it.

BUT WHAT HAPPENS NEXT?

For many speakers, the moment after applause is a strange mix of elation and emptiness. The high of the stage fades, and then—silence. No surge of new clients. No sudden wave of emails. Just the same inbox you left behind.

I've been there. I used to believe that simply showing up authentically and delivering value would be enough, that clients would naturally come pouring in. And for a moment, it felt true. People laughed; they told me my talk shifted their perspective, and I walked away feeling unstoppable. But the glow faded quickly. Days passed, and the silence was deafening. No calls. No new clients. Just me, wondering what I was missing.

A standing ovation may feel like the peak, but it's really the starting line. The applause is proof that you made an impact in the room, but without the right systems, that impact rarely carries beyond the event.

That's where most speakers stop, but that's where your opportunity begins.

What if, instead of fading, the energy of that moment was captured, nurtured, and multiplied? What if you had a structure in place that transformed applause into ongoing conversations, inquiries, and clients?

That's what this next section is all about.

We'll pull back the curtain on the systems that turn your talk from a single moment into a lasting movement. You'll see how:

- Your **website** becomes your digital stage, guiding the right people forward.
- Your **funnels** extend the applause, keeping the conversation alive.
- Your **backend systems** quietly handle the details, so no lead slips through the cracks.

Just like music, where the encore lingers long after the last note, these systems make sure your message keeps playing in the minds and inboxes of the people who need it most.

Your Digital Stage: A Website That Converts

Your website isn't meant to entertain everyone who stops by. It's meant to warmly guide the right people forward. Think of it as the encore to your talk, a space for those who aren't ready for the conversation to end.

When you're on stage, your talk is structured. You open strong, tell stories that land, and close with a call to action. Your website should do the exact same thing.

Too often, speakers treat their site like a business card, something to hand out but not something that truly works for them. Your website is your digital stage, and every visitor is another chance to keep the mic in your hand.

Common Mistakes Speakers Make

For years, I had a beautiful website, crisp design, professional photos, and a clever tagline. But it wasn't doing its job. It didn't convert or guide people anywhere. When someone heard me speak and typed my URL, they ended up wandering rather than moving forward. It was like delivering an amazing talk, then walking offstage, leaving the audience unsure what to do next.

Confused people don't buy, so you must create a clear path for your audience. Ask yourself, *What action do I want someone to take when they land on my website after hearing me speak?* Without that direction, even the most powerful talk will end in silence. The moment you define the next step and guide people toward it, everything changes.

What My Website Includes Now

- **A Strong Call-to-Action Above the Fold** – so visitors immediately know the next step to take, without scrolling or guessing. ("Above the fold" simply means the part of your website that people see first, before they scroll. It's prime real estate, the spot that grabs attention and sets the tone. If you don't make the next step clear here, many visitors will click away before exploring further.)

- **A Dedicated Speaker Page** – showcasing my topics, past events, testimonials, and a simple way for event planners to book me.

- **Lead Capture With Email Integration** – every download, inquiry, or sign-up goes straight into my CRM, so I can follow up automatically and never lose a lead.

- **Social Proof** – from client testimonials to logos of organizations I've worked with, building trust and credibility at a glance.

A great digital stage sets the scene, but the show can't stop there. Once someone leaves your site, you need a way to carry them deeper. That's where your funnel comes in.

YOUR INVISIBLE STAGE CREW: POST-TALK SALES FUNNELS

Your funnel isn't about being pushy. It's your gentle encore invitation, the way you whisper, "I see you, I value you," long after the mic is put away.

Every speaker knows you can't pull off an event alone. Behind the curtain, there's a crew making sure everything flows seamlessly. Most of the audience never sees them, but without that team, the show would fall flat.

Your business works the same way. While you're off on your next adventure, you need a behind-the-scenes system running the show, responding to leads, and keeping the momentum alive.

SO, WHAT IS A FUNNEL REALLY?

The word "funnel" gets a bad rap. It sounds mechanical and boring. Let's flip the narrative: a funnel is simply a guided encore experience.

MY FUNNEL FLOW

Here's what happens after I step off stage:

- **A Landing Page With an Opt-In** – I direct the audience to a simple page where they can grab a free resource, join my list, or learn more. No distractions, just one clear action.

- **A Warm Welcome Email** – As soon as they sign up, they get an email that thanks them for connecting, reminds them who I am, and delivers exactly what I promised.

- **A Short Nurture Sequence** – Over the next few days, they receive a handful of emails that build trust, share value, and show them how I can help beyond the stage.

- **A Clear Next Step** – Whether it's booking a call, exploring services, or inviting me to speak again, the path forward is obvious. No guesswork, no crickets, just momentum.

Why it matters: Funnels extend the applause into meaningful connections and sales.

Speakers Edge: If you can connect with attendees before the event, do it! Think of it like the opening band. They set the tone, warm up the crowd, and build excitement. By engaging early, you're already creating anticipation for your message.

WHAT TO LOOK FOR IN A FUNNEL TOOL

- **Automatic Tagging and Segmentation** – So each subscriber goes to the right list without manual sorting.

- **Personal-Feeling Automation** – Emails that sound like you wrote them one by one.

- **Easy Nurture Sequence Builder** – Visual, drag-and-drop tools that let you map out the journey without needing a tech degree.

- **Clear Tracking and Insights** – Like watching your audience in real time, you can see who opened, clicked, and converted.

Funnels nurture relationships after the event. But to even get people into your funnel, you need to capture their details in the moment.

THE ROADIES WHO NEVER SLEEP: SCALING WITH BACKEND SYSTEMS

Think of your backend system as your roadie. Just like a roadie makes sure your slides are ready and your water is waiting on stage, your system handles the behind-the-scenes details, capturing leads, sending follow-ups, and keeping momentum alive.

These systems don't replace your message; they multiply it, transforming one moment on stage into countless points of connection. With the right system in place, no one slips through the cracks, and every opportunity is nurtured. You're not just delivering a great talk; you're turning applause into lasting results.

Picture this: you've just finished a keynote. Dozens of people want to connect. Instead of fumbling with business cards or hoping they remember your name, your system goes to work.

Your website acts as the digital replay of your stage. Your funnels guide people to a clear next step. Your CRM captures and nurtures every lead. Your appointment scheduler makes it effortless to book time with you.

The momentum doesn't stop when you step off stage; your systems keep carrying it forward.

What Scaling with Systems Really Looks Like

- **From One Stage to Many** – A single keynote becomes a webinar, a course, or a nurture sequence because your systems repurpose content.

- **Consistent Client Experience** – Whether someone met you in Phoenix, at breakfast, or online, every lead enters the same streamlined journey.

- **Freedom to Focus** – Instead of chasing tasks, your backend runs the show. You get to prepare your next talk or simply rest.

What to Look for in Backend Systems (Your CRM as the Backstage Crew)

When the spotlight is on you, your focus should be the audience, not juggling details. That's where your CRM steps in, acting as your backstage crew to keep the show running seamlessly long after you've left the stage.

- **All-in-One Functionality** – Like a stage manager, your CRM unites scheduling, automation, tagging, invoicing, and more, so nothing gets lost behind the curtain.

- **Simple, Smart Workflows** – Picture this: someone opts in on your landing page → they're tagged in your CRM → a personalized email sequence welcomes them → you're notified to follow up. Just like a backstage crew hitting their cues, everything flows without you lifting a finger.

- **Always Working, Even When You're Not** – On stage, on a plane, or on a break, your CRM keeps capturing leads, sending reminders, and nurturing connections in the background.

- **Consistency That Builds Trust** – Just as every performance follows a script, your CRM delivers a smooth, professional experience to every client, building confidence and loyalty.

- **Scalable by Design** – Whether you're speaking once or a hundred times, your CRM grows with you: capturing leads before, during, and after your talk, automating media kit delivery, tracking prospects, and repeating what works, like a touring show that gets better with every stop.

- **Backstage Tip** – Think of your website and CRM as co-presenters: your website is the always-open replay of your stage, while your CRM is the stage manager making sure everyone gets exactly what they need.

Bottom line: Scaling isn't about doing more, it's about doing less, better. With the right systems in place, every stage becomes a springboard to greater reach, deeper impact, and more clients without burnout.

Why it matters: This is how one talk = multiple clients + more speaking invitations.

And the best part is that you don't have to piece together dozens of tools to make this happen. That's where WalkHer CRM steps in, your all-in-one backstage pass.

Your Backstage Pass: WalkHer CRM for Speakers

By now, you've seen how systems keep the conversation alive after the stage. But you might be wondering, *What system can actually do all this without overwhelming me?*

That's why I started my agency, **The WalkHer CRM powered by Go High Level.**

This isn't just another software tool. It's a comprehensive platform designed specifically for speakers, coaches, and service providers who are ready to scale with ease.

Instead of piecing together multiple apps, WalkHer CRM serves as your behind-the-scenes support team, streamlining operations, automating workflows, and keeping everything running smoothly. That way, you can stay focused on delivering your expertise and shining in front of your audience.

Here's What It Makes Possible:

- **Websites and Landing Pages That Convert** – a polished home base that turns audiences into leads
- **Real-Time Lead Capture** – text-to-opt-in, QR codes, and forms that tag and segment automatically
- **Seamless Automation** – email sequences, tagging, reminders, and workflows
- **Booking and Scheduling Tools** – calendars, intake forms, confirmations—no chasing people down
- **Full Client Journey Tracking** – from the moment they hear you speak to the day they book you again
- **Scalable, Repeatable Processes** – so every event feels smooth and stress-free

The real reason I recommend WalkHer CRM isn't just the features. It's the freedom it creates. It allows me to step off stage knowing the encore is already in motion.

The True Encore Effect

Beautiful speaker, let's end where we began, with you on stage, standing in your power. The lights dim, the applause rises, and in that moment, you know you've given your all.

But here's the gift: your talk doesn't have to end when you step off stage.

Your voice is the spark. Your systems are the force that carries it forward. Together, they create the encore—the part that lingers, the tune people hum on the way home, the words that echo in their minds long after the room is empty.

We've walked through what it takes to make that encore possible:

- **Your Digital Stage: A Website That Converts** – the place where your audience lands when the spotlight fades
- **Your Invisible Stage Crew: Post-Talk Funnels** – quietly working behind the scenes to guide your audience from applause to action
- **The Roadies Who Never Sleep: Scalable Backend Systems** – keeping the show running smoothly while multiplying your message

Start small. Add a clear call to action to your website. Record a short welcome video. Create a simple landing page just for event organizers. Each step is a note in the melody of your encore.

And when it all comes together, you'll realize the standing ovation was never the finale; it was only the beginning. Because when you build systems that sell, your talk keeps speaking long after the applause fades, carrying your brilliance into inboxes, conversations, communities, and client calls.

That's the true encore effect: your voice amplified, your message multiplied, your impact sustained.

Ready for Your Next Step?

Let WalkHer CRM (www.walkhercrm.com) be your backstage pass. It's the all-in-one system designed to capture the magic of your talks and carry it forward with ease. I'd love to invite you to explore how it can support your journey, so you can keep shining on stage while your systems keep the encore alive.

Ready to Turn Applause into Clients?

Discover the Secret System Top Speakers Use to Keep the Conversation Going

Scan the QR Code to access:

☑ Capture leads live during your talks (with QR or text-to-opt-in tools)
☑ Build automated follow-ups that book clients while you're offstage
☑ Design a website + funnel that work 24/7
☑ Create systems that turn every event into ongoing revenue

Ready to Keep the Encore Alive?

Download your free copy of ***The Speaker's Encore Workbook*** and start turning your talks into a repeatable, automated client system today.

Tracy Walker

TW Creative Design

www.twreativedesign.com

 @twcreativedesign

@tracy-walker-twcd

Tracy Walker is the tech-savvy, systems-loving strategist behind TW Creative Design! As an entrepreneur, speaker, and digital powerhouse, Tracy helps creative business owners ditch the overwhelm and build websites and systems that work for you. With over 32 years of customer service know-how and a knack for streamlining chaos, she turns "tech tangles" into smooth, scalable solutions.

Whether you're stuck in content creation overload or knee-deep in launch stress, Tracy's your go-to guide for clarity, structure, and sustainable growth. When she's not organizing digital empires, you'll find her empowering entrepreneurs to stop duct-taping their business together and start thriving with smart strategy.

<u>Education, Certifications, & Accreditations</u>

- BS from Iowa State University
- Website Development & Design Certification from Des Moines Area Community College
- Emotional Intelligence Graduate from Boston Breakthrough Academy
- Leadership Training from Boston Breakthrough Academy
- Go High Level Technical Training (Admin Certification in progress)
- Marketing Certification through The Gold Digger Girl

4

Relationships, Not Reach: The Real ROI of Speaking
by Molly Ruland

It was a Tuesday, coffee in hand, inbox open, and I was halfway through my morning ritual of aggressively deleting emails when one came through that made me stop cold. A client—let's call her Miss Metrics—had just sent me her new podcast guesting criteria: "If the show doesn't have at least 7,500 downloads per episode, it's not worth my time." Seven. Thousand. Five. Hundred. She might as well have told me she was holding out for the Vatican to call. Mind you, she has zero social media presence, a brand-new company with a co-founder who left sixty days in, and no track record whatsoever.

Not to mention that if a podcast gets 7,500 downloads in the first month, that puts it in the top 1 percent of all podcasts, which makes it technically bananas that Miss Metrics thought that was the bare minimum she would accept. Ma'am, I'm going to need you to take a seat, maybe a few of them.

I stared blankly at the message, thinking, *Am I being punked?* My first reaction wasn't even frustration; it was curiosity. No, I'm lying, I was annoyed AF. But also, had I failed so spectacularly at setting expectations that we'd reduced the value of human conversation to a download count? I mean, sure, we live in a world where metrics matter. Open rates, click-throughs, views—I get it. But if you're a small business owner with a service-based business, those numbers don't pay your bills. *People* do. Downloads don't close deals. *Relationships* do.

I took a sip of what I wished was Irish coffee and muttered to myself, "Where did we go wrong?" That question would become the seed for everything that followed.

I've been in business long enough to see how easily "visibility" turns into a monster we end up serving instead of directing. The obsession with metrics makes sense; it's comforting to have numbers to point to when the emotional roller coaster of entrepreneurship is, well, roller-coastering. But somewhere along the way, we quietly swapped connection for reach. We started chasing exposure instead of alignment, status instead of synergy. We started "twerking for the algo" and totally lost the plot. Don't believe me, look at social media.

And here's the real kicker—most people don't even realize they're doing it. They'll say things like: "I just need more traffic to my site." "I need to grow my audience before launching." "I need to get on bigger shows." But often what they *really* need is to nurture the relationships right in front of them. Because the truth is that you don't need the whole internet to buy from you; you just need the right people to trust you. I'm willing to bet that if you got one hundred new clients tomorrow, it would be a serious issue, a seriously bad one. One hundred new clients in one day could bankrupt you. You don't want to go viral. Trust me. Would one new client a month change your business? It would change mine; that's for sure. So, let's start small and stay realistic.

Let's pause for a reality check about podcast guesting. You might think getting on podcasts is the modern way to "speak your way to sales"—and it is—but not because of some mystical funnel hidden in the audio waves. Podcasting is expensive. It's time-intensive. You need equipment, editing, and preferably a mic that doesn't sound like you're calling in from a tuna can. And if you plan to hop on someone's show, drop your offer, collect fans, and peace out, you're missing the point of why the medium works at all.

You are not there to extract. You are there to connect.

I've seen how this plays out when people miss that memo. One of my clients had a guest who, mid-recording, said, "Hold on, I have to spit." Yes—*during the interview.* Because he was at the dentist! We later joked that he should've titled his episode "Don't Be This Guy." But beyond the absurdity of it all, that experience taught me something bigger. There's an invisible moment that happens with every host—the moment they decide whether to root for you long-term. Just like on dating apps, we all know in moments if it's a swipe left or right; business relationships aren't any different. Miss my recording with no email, you're dead to me; I don't care how many social media followers you have. You just showed me how you work, and I believe you.

That moment has nothing to do with how clever your talking points are. It's about respect. Professionalism is a form of marketing. Enthusiasm is a selling strategy. Care is currency. You never know which hosts will go on to become partners, advocates, or friends. I always remind my clients: when you're a guest, you are borrowing someone's digital house. Be the kind of guest who gets invited back. Those podcast hosts have thousands of relationships that could change your life forever. Forget the audience; the only one who matters is the host.

See, a few months before Miss Metrics slapped me upside the head with her unrealistic expectations, I was invited to be a guest on *The Power Lounge,* hosted by Amy Vaughan from Together Digital. Now, this is the point where most "growth hackers" would smirk. The show averages around a hundred listens per episode—not seven thousand. Not even seven hundred. One hundred. You know what I said? "Absolutely. Let's do it."

I didn't run audience demographics or check conversion rates. I wanted to talk to her, not her analytics. That conversation turned out to be one of the most pivotal hours of my business life because Amy is smart, kind, and purposeful, and I am so glad that's how I made my decision. Amy later invited me to teach a masterclass for her community. That one event introduced me to dozens of powerhouse women in digital marketing, people I'd go on to collaborate with, travel with, partner with, and laugh with over the occasional glass (fine, bottle) of wine. Within months, my calendar filled, my business expanded, and I was being introduced to opportunities I hadn't even imagined when I agreed to be on that podcast.

The show didn't have a viral audience. But it had the right audience. That's the thing people forget about numbers—the power isn't in how *many* see you, but *who* sees you. Connections create compounding returns. A podcast might have one hundred listeners, but if one of them is the right connector, the right collaborator, the right champion—congratulations, you've just made your quarter.

Here's what I've learned from years of speaking, hosting, and guesting: your pipeline is people. Every opportunity in my business has come from a *who*, not a *how*. It wasn't an algorithm that got me to new stages; it was someone who'd seen me speak and said, "You'd be perfect for this." Relationships build leverage because trust travels faster than marketing does. And unlike social media, relationships don't expire when the algorithm changes.

In fact, one of my now best friends on the entire planet, Katie Nelson, was introduced to me this way, and we have been besties ever since. My life has been infinitely better in more ways than I can count because of Katie Nelson, and it all started at a NAWBO event, of course. Someone told her I was speaking and that she would love me, and they were right. Eight years later, I love me some Mrs. Nelson. In fact, when I moved to Costa Rica, Katie let me keep all my stuff in her garage; now that's love. And guess what, she also has a chapter in this book, so you are in luck.

More than once, I've turned down collaborations that looked lucrative on paper but felt misaligned in spirit. At this point in life, I'm allergic to transactional energy. If I don't like the vibe, it's a no from me, dog. No spreadsheet has ever made me laugh until I cried; no KPI brought soup when I was sick. So yes, I love a good strategy. But underneath every one of mine sits a message that sounds something like: work with good humans. That's the heartbeat of everything I do. In fact, my company is called Heartcast Media. I didn't name it that to work with wankers.

Business ownership gives you a special kind of privilege—the freedom to choose your people. That's not just about picking dream clients; it's about intentionally curating your circle. Maybe it's perimenopause, or maybe it's just good business; either way, I am not impressed by vanity metrics; it's a trap. I tell people all the time: alignment isn't woo-woo; it's efficiency. When you spend your time with people who energize you, you get more creative, generous, and magnetic.

And the reason podcast guesting is so powerful is that you get to demonstrate who you are in real time. People can hear your tone, humor, and philosophy. They see how you think. They get a taste of what it's like to work with you without the sales pitch. That's what sells. Not your "three-step framework." You. The best way to show people how you work is to show people how you work. It's really that simple. If you can make people laugh, you probably have a lot of childhood trauma, and you just might be really good at sales. And by you, I mean me.

The truest form of speaking your way to sales is showing up as your full, unfakeable self in front of real human beings, again and again, until familiarity turns into trust, and trust turns into collaboration, and collaboration turns into income. Be yourself; don't hold back. My best interviews were the ones where the polish wore off, and the real me came out, for better or worse. I come from a long line of orators, bartenders, and bootleggers. We love a stage, and the Irish have a way of telling you to go to hell in such a way that you will enjoy the trip. The closer I get to fifty, the less filter I have and the more my business has grown. My backup plan is stand-up comedy. I am probably a lot of people's "most ridiculous friend," and I am 100 percent okay with that. Embrace your quirks, lean into them, show your experience, forget the polish. Pretend you are at a wedding in line to get a drink, and you are chatting with someone; that's how you win this game. Whenever I get the opportunity to speak publicly, I am positive that some people leave the room feeling like they need to pray for me, and other people "freaking love me," and I'm totally okay with that.

If you were to chart a "relationship ROI," it would never look linear. There's no formula that says one podcast appearance equals five leads. What you get instead is a web of connections that grows in depth and density over time. It's the host who introduces you to another host. It's the audience member who becomes a referral partner months later. It's the loyal listener who doesn't hire you right away—but five posts, three episodes, and one speaking event later, says, "Okay, I'm ready."

Here's what else happens: your friends start making money, too. That's the beautiful ripple effect of doing business relationally; you lift as you climb. That's what happened after *The Power Lounge.* That collaboration with Amy snowballed into our *Together Marketing Rescue* podcast, supported by Goldman Sachs. That partnership has generated measurable revenue for women-owned businesses and more joy than I can quantify.

Most importantly, never forget to nurture the relationship: follow up after the recording, post the clips on your social media and tag them, and send an email to introduce them to someone. Build some freaking value for crying out loud. Don't just one-and-done them like a bad Tinder date. Don't ghost your podcast hosts; it's just rude and super shortsighted. That host could change your life forever, and all you have to do is be a human. Wild concept, right?

And somewhere, I imagine Miss Metrics is still chasing download charts, wondering why the likes aren't converting. Meanwhile, the rest of us are out here building something solid and sustainable: trust.

If I could whisper one thing into the ears of every entrepreneur starting out, it would be this: you don't need to be famous. You need to be trusted. Speaking—especially podcasting—is one of the most human ways to earn that trust. It's intimate. It's messy sometimes— your dog barks, your kid walks in—but it's real. And that realness is what draws people to you. Not perfection. Not polish. Don't get me wrong, though, buy a microphone, ya heathens. What is this, 2019? Sound does matter; trust me. And for the love of sound, don't even think about buying a Yeti.

When you treat every conversation like an opportunity to connect rather than convert, you become unforgettable—and eventually, unstoppable.

So, the next time you're tempted to say no to a speaking opportunity because "the numbers are too small," imagine me shaking my head at you, fists in the air, muttering something unprintable but loving. Downloads matter. Metrics matter. But relationships? Relationships matter more because they are forever.

That's how you truly speak your way to sales. Not by shouting louder, but by listening deeper. Not by hunting audiences, but by tending friendships. And sometimes by saying yes to the tiny podcast that changes everything.

Scan this to get access to my "always a yes" list of podcasts

Scan the QR Code to access:

☑ 15% off just for reading
Speak Your Way to Sales

www.proposals.heartcastmedia.com/special-offer

Molly Ruland

Heartcast Media

heartcastmedia.com

Molly has helmed her multimedia companies for over two decades and is now a trailblazer in the branded podcast production realm. Based in DC but managing her operations from Costa Rica, Molly's expertise spans producing top-ranking podcasts across various genres. Her client roster is impressively diverse, encompassing the Department of Health, DC Government, NATO, dating coaches, and former NBA players, consistently delivering high-quality, strategic, branded content across the board.

Under Molly's leadership, Heartcast Media has become synonymous with premier branded podcast production, aiding businesses in boosting revenue and fostering strategic relationships over the last 6 years. With a deep understanding of podcasting dynamics, content creation, and guest booking, Molly is a sought-after speaker who brings valuable insights to every engagement.

Living next to a volcano in Costa Rica with her three dogs, she embodies the philosophy that "listening is the revolution," driving her global business forward with passion and innovation. Prospect Clip is an extension of the work she has done for years by enabling sales teams of all capabilities and levels.

5

STOP CHASING GIGS, START ATTRACTING THEM: THE PR PLAYBOOK FOR SPEAKERS
BY HEATHER MCELRATH

INTRODUCTION

You deliver a strong talk, the audience is engaged, the feedback is positive—and then nothing. No new invitations, no client inquiries, no ripple effect beyond the room. Many speakers experience this frustrating gap: they're skilled on stage but struggle to translate that visibility into ongoing opportunities.

That gap isn't solved by piling on more speaking gigs; it's solved by amplifying the ones you already have. This is where public relations (PR) comes in. Most speakers assume PR is reserved for celebrities, Fortune 500 executives, or people with big agencies behind them. In truth, PR is the practical engine that builds the credibility and visibility event planners are looking for when they're deciding who to book next.

The speaking market has shifted. Planners don't just rely on referrals or bureaus; they Google potential speakers, scroll LinkedIn, and look for third-party validation before making a decision. They want experts who already show up in respected places: quoted in industry publications, interviewed on podcasts, or featured in event previews. PR gives you that edge.

In this chapter, we'll demystify PR for speakers: why earned coverage outperforms ads for credibility, how to position yourself as the go-to expert in your niche, and how AI has made professional-level PR accessible without a massive budget. By the end, you'll understand how to generate consistent media coverage, turn that visibility into more speaking invitations, and use modern tools to manage PR like a pro. Not to become famous, just to become the obvious choice when event planners need an expert voice.

What is Public Relations?

Let's start with what public relations actually is, because most speakers (most people) have the wrong idea entirely.

Public relations is the strategic process of managing how your target audience perceives you through earned credibility rather than paid advertising. When a journalist quotes you in an article, when a podcast host interviews you about industry trends, or when a trade publication features your expertise—that's PR in action. It's the art and science of getting other people to tell your story for you.

Here's the crucial distinction many speakers miss: PR is fundamentally different from marketing. Marketing involves paying for attention. For example, buying ads, sponsoring posts, or purchasing speaking directory listings. Marketing drives direct action: "Hire me for your next event." PR, on the other hand, earns attention and builds your reputation. It positions you as someone worth listening to before event planners even know they need you.

Think of it this way: when you see an ad for a speaker, you know they paid to be there. When you see that same speaker quoted as an expert in Forbes or interviewed on a popular podcast, you assume they earned that placement through credibility and expertise. That assumption is the power of PR.

For speakers specifically, PR serves as your credibility multiplier. Every media mention, every expert quote, every podcast appearance doesn't just reach a new audience. It signals to event planners that other professionals consider you worth featuring. It's third-party validation at scale.

The key PR tools that matter most for speakers include:

- **Media Coverage:** Getting quoted, interviewed, or featured in articles relevant to your expertise. These could include national publications, industry trade magazines, or even well-respected local outlets.

- **Thought Leadership:** Writing guest articles, op-eds, or expert commentary that positions you as someone who shapes industry conversation rather than just commenting on it.

- **Podcasts:** Regular appearances on shows in your niche, which often have highly engaged audiences and long shelf lives.

- **Awards and Recognition:** Industry honors, certifications, or recognition that create natural PR opportunities and speaking credentials.

- **Speaking-Specific PR:** Coverage in event industry publications, speaker bureau features, or conference preview articles that put you directly in front of event planners.

Common PR Mistakes That Kill Your Chances

Before diving into successful PR strategies, let's address the mistakes that sabotage most speakers' media efforts. Understanding what doesn't work is just as important as knowing what does, especially since these errors are so common that avoiding them instantly puts you ahead of 90 percent of other speakers trying to get media attention.

The "Spray and Pray" Fallacy

The biggest mistake speakers make is assuming that volume equals results. They send generic press releases to hundreds of outlets, believing that casting the widest possible net will somehow generate coverage. This "spray and pray" approach is not only ineffective, but it's also counterproductive.

Mass outreach with generic pitches signals to journalists that you don't understand their audience or beat. When a cybersecurity expert sends the same pitch to a fashion magazine, a local sports reporter, and a business podcast, it demonstrates a fundamental misunderstanding of how media works. Journalists receive hundreds of irrelevant pitches daily; yours just adds to the noise.

The truth is counterintuitive: the more targeted and specific your outreach, the higher your success rate. It's better to send ten highly personalized pitches to carefully selected outlets than one hundred generic emails to random publications.

IGNORING THE POWER OF LOCAL MEDIA

Speakers consistently overlook their most accessible opportunity: local media outlets. They chase national publications while ignoring regional business journals, local TV morning shows, and community newspapers that are actively seeking expert sources.

Local media offers several advantages that national outlets don't. Local journalists are more likely to respond because you're part of their community. Local angles make stories more relevant to their audiences. And local coverage often leads to bigger opportunities; national outlets frequently pick up stories that start locally.

Even if you're speaking at an event across the country, your local connection gives you credibility. A Washington, DC-based cybersecurity expert has a better chance with DC business publications than with Los Angeles outlets, even if the speaking event is in LA. The local angle creates natural relevance.

MISUNDERSTANDING BEAT SYSTEMS

Journalists aren't generalists; they're specialists assigned to specific "beats" or subject areas. A crime reporter doesn't cover business stories. A wellness journalist isn't interested in technology trends. Yet speakers routinely pitch random journalists without understanding their coverage areas.

If you speak about sales, you want to reach business reporters who cover entrepreneurship, small business, or corporate news. Suppose your expertise is workplace wellness; target journalists who write about health, human resources, or workplace culture. This basic research step dramatically improves your response rates.

You can easily identify a journalist's beat by scanning their recent articles or checking their social media bio. Most journalists clearly indicate their coverage areas so sources can pitch them relevant stories.

Forgetting That Timing Creates News

Having expertise isn't enough; you need to connect that expertise to what's happening now. Speakers often pitch their general knowledge without tying it to current events, trending topics, or timely issues their audience cares about.

The news operates on eight key principles that determine what gets coverage, and understanding these can transform your pitch success:

- **Timeliness:** Your angle must be happening now or address recent developments. That sales expert we mentioned earlier shouldn't just pitch "sales tips;" they should pitch "how to maintain sales momentum during economic uncertainty" when that's the current concern.

- **Impact:** How many people does your insight affect? "Leadership tips" is vague, but "why 70 percent of remote teams are failing at leadership transition" suggests broad relevance.

- **Proximity:** Stories that affect the local audience get priority. Frame your expertise around local implications of broader trends.

- **Prominence:** If you've worked with recognizable companies or have notable credentials, mention them. "Former Apple executive explains innovation strategy" carries more weight than generic expertise claims.

- **Conflict:** Disagreement creates interest. Can you offer a contrarian view on popular business wisdom? Do you challenge conventional thinking in your field?

- **Human Interest:** Personal stories that illustrate broader issues resonate with audiences. That sales expert who learned door-to-door selling as a child has a compelling human interest angle.

- **Oddity:** Unusual backgrounds, unexpected career paths, or surprising insights make you memorable. The cybersecurity expert who was formerly a hacker has built in intrigue.

- **Progress:** Can you speak to emerging trends, new developments, or positive changes in your industry?

PITCHING YOURSELF INSTEAD OF PROVIDING VALUE

The most fundamental mistake speakers make is approaching PR as self-promotion rather than value creation. They lead with their credentials, speaking topics, and availability, rather than what they can offer the journalist's audience.

Compare these approaches:

- **Wrong:** "I'm a leadership speaker with fifteen years of experience and over two hundred presentations. I'm available for interviews about my upcoming book."

- **Right:** "With layoffs hitting the tech sector, I can provide expert commentary on how leaders should communicate difficult decisions to retain team trust and productivity."

The first pitch is about you. The second is about solving a problem the journalist's audience faces. Journalists don't care about your speaking career; they care about serving their readers, listeners, or viewers.

Failing to Follow Up (Or Following Up Too Much)

Speakers either send a single pitch and wait forever for a response, or bombard journalists with daily follow-ups that border on harassment. Both approaches kill your chances.

The sweet spot is professional persistence: one follow-up after a week, perhaps a second follow-up with a new angle after another week, then moving on. If a journalist doesn't respond after two thoughtful attempts, they're not interested, and continued outreach will only damage your reputation.

Not Leveraging What You Already Have

Many speakers sit on goldmines of PR-worthy content without realizing it. Client success stories become case studies. Industry observations become expert commentary. Speaking experiences become trend analysis.

That testimonial saying your presentation "transformed our company culture" can become "Local expert's methodology helps Fortune 500 company achieve 40 percent improvement in employee engagement." You're not fabricating news; you're presenting existing achievements in newsworthy ways.

Treating PR as a One-Time Campaign

The most common strategic failure is treating PR as a short-term, one-time activity rather than a consistent system. Many speakers will try it for a month, get discouraged by the initial lack of results, and then quit. They fail to understand that media relationships and credibility are built over time. Each pitch, each connection, and each piece of coverage builds momentum for the next one. The speakers who truly succeed are those who commit to consistent effort over months, not just a few days.

Why PR Matters for Speakers

The speaking industry operates on a simple principle: event planners hire experts they trust and recognize. In a crowded market where thousands of qualified speakers compete for attention, PR solves the fundamental challenge of obscurity and builds that trust at scale.

What separates the speakers who are consistently booked from those who struggle isn't always better content; it's a combination of visibility and credibility. When a planner searches for a leadership expert, they are looking for an authority. The speaker who has been quoted in business journals, appeared on industry podcasts, and written for trade publications will always have a decisive advantage over an equally talented but invisible peer.

This is where you see the virtuous cycle of PR in action; a process that creates a powerful compound effect on your speaking career. It works like this:

A single media mention leads to a podcast interview. That interview gets you noticed by an event planner, resulting in a speaking invitation. The talk you give then generates new stories and data to pitch, which leads to even better media coverage, which in turn attracts higher-paying gigs. Each win doesn't just add to your resume; it multiplies the opportunities and authority that follow.

The result of this cycle is the transformation of your business from constant outbound prospecting (you chasing planners) to consistent inbound opportunities (planners discovering you).

Beyond generating leads, PR enhances every marketing tool in your arsenal. Your speaker reel becomes more compelling with "As Seen In" logos from credible publications. Your website bio carries more weight when it lists recent media appearances. Even your email pitches are more effective when you can reference your status as a featured expert. This third-party validation is unparalleled. When you say you're an expert, it's marketing. When a respected media outlet features you as an expert, it's proof.

How PR Works

Effective public relations isn't about luck; it's an engine you can build. It follows a predictable, four-step process that transforms you from an unknown speaker into a recognized expert. Here is the system that will separate you from the speakers who get lucky once and turn you into one who builds sustained visibility.

Step 1: Define Your Message and Niche

Before you pitch anyone, you need to be clear on two things: who you serve and what unique perspective you bring to the table. This isn't about limiting yourself; it's about making yourself memorable and quotable.

Start by identifying your core audience. Are you speaking to corporate executives about leadership? Healthcare professionals about patient experience? Entrepreneurs about scaling businesses? The more specific you can be, the easier it becomes to identify relevant media outlets and craft compelling pitches.

Next, define your expert voice: the unique angle that makes you different from other speakers in your space. Maybe you're the cyber-security expert who spent twenty years as a reformed hacker. Or the leadership speaker who built three companies before age thirty. Or the customer service expert who turned around failing call centers. Your angle becomes your hook for media attention.

Step 2: Build Your Media List

Effective PR starts with knowing exactly which journalists, podcasters, and editors cover topics related to your expertise. The key is building relationships with the right people who regularly need expert sources.

Focus your research on industry-specific outlets, business publications that cover your topic area, podcasts in your niche, and even local media that might be interested in your unique story or regional angle. Trade publications are often overlooked but can be incredibly valuable because they have engaged audiences and are always seeking expert commentary.

Don't ignore local opportunities. Regional business journals, local TV morning shows, and community newspapers frequently need expert sources for national stories with local angles. These outlets often provide easier entry points for building your media presence.

Step 3: Pitch Yourself

Here's where most speakers go wrong: they pitch themselves as speakers rather than as expert sources. Effective PR pitches offer value to journalists or hosts, not a sales pitch for your speaking services.

Your pitch should be short, relevant, and value driven. Instead of "I'm available to speak at events," try "I can provide expert commentary on the cybersecurity implications of the recent data breach trend." Instead of promoting your credentials, offer insights that help the journalist tell a better story.

Strong pitch angles typically fall into three categories: industry trends you can explain or predict, personal stories that illustrate broader issues, or solutions to problems that affect the publication's audience. The key is leading with what you can give, not what you want to get.

Step 4: Repurpose and Promote

Once you land media coverage, your work isn't done; it's just beginning. Every PR win should feed your broader marketing efforts and create opportunities for additional coverage.

Share media mentions across all your platforms. Add "As Seen In" logos to your website and speaker materials. Reference recent coverage in future pitches to establish credibility. Update your LinkedIn profile and email signature. Create social media content that amplifies the coverage to your audience.

Each piece of coverage also becomes a launching pad for additional PR opportunities. Use recent articles as credibility builders in pitches to other outlets. Reference podcast appearances when reaching out to conference organizers. Turn media quotes into speaker bio updates that attract event planners.

Quick PR Wins for Speakers

Ready to implement PR strategies immediately? Here's your quick-start checklist for generating media coverage and building credibility without waiting months for results.

Start with Your Foundation

Draft a professional speaker bio that emphasizes your expertise rather than your speaking credentials. Instead of "John has delivered over one hundred presentations," write "John has helped Fortune 500 companies reduce cybersecurity incidents by 40 percent through his proprietary risk assessment framework." Media outlets want to quote experts, not speakers.

Create three to five different pitch angles based on your expertise. If you speak about leadership, your angles might include: remote team management trends, generational differences in workplace communication, crisis leadership lessons from recent events, the psychology of decision-making under pressure, and leadership mistakes that destroy company culture. Having multiple angles ready allows you to respond quickly to trending news or journalist requests.

Target Low-Hanging Fruit

Identify ten podcasts in your niche and research their recent episodes to understand their format and guest preferences. Many podcast hosts actively seek expert guests and are more accessible than traditional media outlets. Use AI tools to craft personalized pitches that reference specific episodes and explain how your expertise adds value to their audience.

Your local media represents an often-overlooked opportunity. Regional business journals, local TV morning shows, and community newspapers frequently need expert sources for national stories with local angles. Pitch yourself as the local expert who can comment on industry trends affecting your community.

Leverage What You Already Have

Transform past client testimonials into press-worthy quotes. If a client said your presentation "completely changed how our team approaches customer service," that becomes "According to [Company Name], [Your Name]'s methodology resulted in a complete transformation of their customer service approach." These quasi-case studies provide concrete evidence of your expertise.

Engage strategically on LinkedIn by commenting thoughtfully on industry news and trends. When major developments occur in your field, provide expert commentary that journalists and podcast hosts might notice. Consistent, valuable contributions to industry conversations can lead to media opportunities.

Maximize Every Win

Create a simple system for amplifying media coverage. When you receive any media mention, update your website bio, LinkedIn profile, and email signature immediately. Create social media posts that share the coverage with your network. Add media logos to your speaker one-sheet and presentation materials.

Use each piece of coverage as social proof in future pitches. Opening a pitch with "As recently featured in [Publication], I believe your readers would be interested in…" immediately establishes credibility and increases response rates.

AI-Powered Quick Wins

Use ChatGPT or similar tools to generate pitch templates you can customize for different outlets. Share your expertise and ask for pitch angles that connect your knowledge to current events. AI can help you brainstorm story ideas you might not have considered.

Leverage AI for rapid content creation. Ask it to draft thought leadership article outlines, social media posts promoting your media coverage, or podcast interview talking points. Remember to edit for your authentic voice, but let AI handle the initial heavy lifting.

TRACK AND BUILD MOMENTUM

Keep a simple spreadsheet tracking your media outreach: outlet contacted, pitch sent, response received, coverage secured. This helps you identify which types of pitches work best and which outlets are most responsive to your expertise.

Set a goal of securing one piece of media coverage monthly. This modest target creates consistent visibility without overwhelming your schedule. As you build momentum and relationships, you can increase your activity.

The key to quick PR wins is starting small and building consistently. Even one or two significant media placements can dramatically increase your visibility. A single article quote in a respected publication can generate speaking inquiries for months. A podcast interview can reach thousands of potential clients and event planners. The compound effect of consistent PR effort creates opportunities that transform speaking careers.

You don't need a PR agency to implement these strategies effectively. You need clarity on your message, consistency in your outreach, and the willingness to provide genuine value to journalists and their audiences. AI has made the tactical execution easier than ever, removing the barriers that once limited PR to speakers with substantial budgets.

CONCLUSION AND NEXT STEPS

Public relations isn't about becoming famous; it's about becoming the obvious choice. The speakers who command premium fees and secure the best gigs are not just talented presenters; they are visible authorities. This chapter has shown you that building that authority is no longer a matter of luck or expensive agencies, but a systematic process you can control.

The tools are in your hands, and the playbook is in this chapter. Your next step is not to plan, but to act. Pick one strategy from the PR Toolkit—pitching a local journalist, reaching out to a podcast, or crafting a newsworthy angle with AI—and execute it this week. The speaking industry rewards experts who are both skilled and visible. Go build your visibility.

Heather McElrath

Sandbox Communications

sandboxcom.ai

linkedin.com/in/hmcelrath/

Heather McElrath is the founder of Sandbox Communications, an AI-powered digital marketing and communications agency that helps businesses and thought leaders get seen, heard, and trusted online.

With more than 20 years of experience in public relations and marketing, Heather has guided national associations, fintech innovators, and Fortune 100 brands in strengthening their messaging, visibility, and credibility. Her work blends human strategy with AI speed—bridging traditional PR, digital marketing, and SEO to help organizations connect with confidence.

In *Speak Your Way to Sales*, Heather shares a practical PR playbook for speakers—showing how to turn one-time engagements into ongoing visibility opportunities.

She also teaches PR Essentials at the Borough of Manhattan Community College, helping the next generation of communicators build confidence and career readiness. Heather lives in Chantilly, Va., and enjoys yoga, champagne, and travel.

<u>Education, Certifications, & Accreditations</u>

- MBA, Marketing, The George Washington University
- B.A., Journalism, Virginia Tech
- Leadership Essentials Certificate, Cornell University

6

REPURPOSE TO SELL:
TURNING EVERY TALK
INTO A CONTENT ENGINE
BY KARLYN ANKROM

You've spent weeks, maybe months, preparing that keynote. The research is deep, the stories are sharp, the slides sparkle just enough without screaming "PowerPoint overload." You rehearse in the shower, in the car, maybe even to your dog (who, let's be honest, is your most forgiving audience). Then the big day arrives. You take the stage, deliver with everything you've got, and *boom!* Standing ovation. Mic drop moment.

But here's the question: what happens the next day?

For most speakers, the brilliance that just lit up a ballroom gets packed up with the AV cords and shoved onto a hard drive labeled "Past Talks." Then they move on to the next gig, rinse, repeat, and wonder why their pipeline feels quiet between events.

Here's the truth: your talk isn't a one-and-done performance. It's a content factory waiting to happen.

Every keynote, breakout, or podcast guest spot is raw material for months of social posts, videos, articles, lead magnets, and conversations that keep you visible long after the applause fades. They're the accolades that amplify your authority and boost your bottom line in the "in betweens."

This chapter is your permission slip to stop letting your brilliance gather dust. Instead, let's turn every stage appearance into a visibility machine.

Why Repurposing Is the Speaker's Secret Weapon

We've all heard the saying, "Don't reinvent the wheel." Repurposing is that advice on rocket fuel. You already did the hard work: the research, the rehearsal, the stage delivery (and the many years of experience that got you to this point). Repurposing makes that effort pay off on repeat.

Here's why it matters:

- **People need repetition.** Marketing studies say it takes seven to thirteen touches before someone makes a buying decision. One post about your talk won't cut it. If you're sounding like a broken record to yourself, chances are you're doing it right.

- **You already have the content.** The stories, the stats, the takeaways—they're sitting in your slides and transcripts. Pluck one from your presentation, position it for your audience, and post it.

- **Your audience is busy.** Just because you said it once doesn't mean they heard it, processed it, or remembered it. Repurposing is reinforcement, not redundancy. Your audience needs what you have, and if you don't share it often, you're doing *them* a disservice.

Quick Story: I had a client who wasn't the best at connecting his in-person talks with his digital presence and expertise. He would have people come up to him after his talk to ask questions and inquire about resources, like a book on the topic—except he *wrote* the book on the topic. That's when he realized that the talks weren't enough to make the change in the world he was seeking; he had to lead people into his world before, during, and after the events.

We went back to past podcasts, presentations, books, and articles to repurpose interview clips and knowledge nuggets to elevate his expertise before he hit the next stage. During the event, we positioned him on stage as an authority by making "softball" pitches during his book presentation. Adding phrases like "In my book we dive deeper into this chapter…" and, of course, adding a call-to-action slide asking people to follow him on socials, buy his book, or sign up for his waitlist into his program (p.s. Just one action, never all three). This allowed the audience to continue to deepen their relationship with him long after the talk and gave him deeper insight into audience engagement throughout their journey with his brand. This type of activity led to a waitlist of over five hundred people in just under three weeks.

SHIFT YOUR MINDSET: REPURPOSING ISN'T RECYCLING

Let's clear something up: repurposing doesn't mean reheating leftovers. Though I will say, it can be just as easy.

Repurposing is about context-shifting—same core idea, different frame.

Think of your message as the little black dress of your brand. Oh, la la! On stage, it's paired with heels and statement earrings. On Instagram, it's sneakers and a denim jacket. On LinkedIn, it's a blazer. Same dress, different vibe.

Every platform is just a different room in the same house:

- LinkedIn wants the polished, professional version, with strong stances and expertise elements.

- Instagram craves the behind-the-scenes, relatable vibe with messy action and imperfect prose, which feels a lot like Facetiming your business bestie.

- TikTok thrives on short, snackable moments, with added fun, humor, and a heavy dose of "take me as I am" realness.
- Your email list wants the "pull up a chair and let me tell you a story" tone. Give them the insider scoop, raw opinions, practical advice, and implementation instructions.

Once you stop seeing repurposing as recycling, you realize every talk is a buffet of content waiting to be plated in new ways. And don't worry about getting "caught" repurposing, people don't remember what they had for breakfast this morning, let alone what they saw in their inbox or on social media two weeks ago.

Let's dive into two sample frameworks to get those content creation wheels well-greased and ready to roll, shall we?

FRAMEWORK 1: ONE PAGE, ONE LINE, ONE STORY

Let's start with my favorite system: One Page, One Line, One Story. Yes, this concept is nothing new. You've probably seen versions of "one-liner → storyline" before: scriptwriters turn a logline into scenes and sequences; marketers use Donald Miller's StoryBrand to distill a clear one-liner that expands into websites, emails, and campaigns; fiction writers do it, too, developing a premise into chapters and arcs. We're simply applying that same, proven storytelling pattern to you as a leader marketing your book, talk, or podcast on social media and beyond.

The beauty of this system is that it lets you turn a single page into a quote, a mini-story, and then into a full week of content your future clients want to discuss (complete with compelling CTAs that don't make you sound like a used-car salesperson).

Here's how it works:

1. Take **one page** from your book, talk transcript, or even your slides.
2. Highlight **one line** that pops as a stand-alone idea.

3. Expand that into a **story** that brings the idea to life.

4. That story = one post.

Do that five times, and suddenly you have a week's worth of content from one page. I know, I know. Mind = blown.

Pro Tip: If a line from your keynote got an audible gasp, chuckle, or phones in the air ready to snap a photo of your slide, congratulations, you have repurposing gold. Clip it into a reel. Make it a quote graphic. Tell the same story on LinkedIn with a different CTA. Why should that moment only live in a hotel ballroom when it can live on feeds everywhere? Just sayin'.

FRAMEWORK 2: STRATEGY-TO-STAGE

This one's for the speakers who want maximum mileage from every gig. *Raises hand*

You've already done the hardest part: crafting a message that moves people. Most speakers don't realize that a single talk can fuel a full month of content that nurtures your audience, boosts your credibility, and grows your visibility online.

This isn't about working harder; it's about extracting the full value from work you've already done. This is about working smarter.

Let's zoom in with a pre/during/post event twist.

Think of your talk not just as a forty-five-minute set, but as a three-act play for your visibility:

- **Pre-Event:** Start seeding authority before you ever step on stage. Share behind-the-scenes prep, a "sneak peek" of your slides, or a poll asking your audience what they hope to learn. This builds anticipation and positions you as the expert *before* you even pick up the mic.

    Start documenting your path to the stage well before show week, ideally months or weeks out. If organizers share sample posts or newsletter copy, use them. It saves you time, keeps the event in front of your audience, and reinforces your expertise while reminding followers they might see you there.

Pro Tip: As soon as you're confirmed as a speaker, ask if they'll provide

1. A media kit with sample posts and graphics
2. Ticket codes so you can invite your audience at a special rate or with affiliate perks
3. A recording with Q&A (if you're planning on doing that) of your presentation and how long after you should expect to receive it

- **During the Event:** During the event, capture content in real time: a quick clip of you on stage, a photo with attendees, or a story featuring one of your soundbites. This isn't about selling; it's about giving your wider audience that "wish I was there" feeling. Line up a "content buddy" in the crowd to snap photos and short videos, and if you don't know anyone attending, ask your speaker handler. Also, challenge the audience to take one action during the session—post a takeaway, answer a prompt, or share a photo—and tag you. It builds connections in the room and extends your reach beyond it.

If you've been to any of my presentations, you've probably noticed I don't have a content buddy in the crowd. So, I bake a photo moment into my talk. I've closed sessions by recording a short-form Reel live to show the process and capture the crowd behind me. If your content doesn't lend itself to a selfie, use it as part of the icebreaker and to warm up the crowd. Use a playful line like: "I need a photo for my mom, or she won't believe I spoke here." The final way to bake in the physical-to-digital dot connection is to wrap it up with an ending slide that makes the next step easy: your social handles, a scannable QR code, and an invite to follow along with your journey. Whether it's a planned reel or a selfie from the stage, you'll walk away with content, credibility, and proof of the audience you just energized.

- **Post-Event:** Post-event is where the momentum builds. Share testimonials, audience takeaways, and turn Q&A into fresh posts. Engage with your audience who followed you or tagged you in their event content, and reply with appreciation and a question like, "What's your biggest question about [topic]?" to keep the conversation going.

  Reshare the organizers' recap video if they post one, and add a quick takeaway you had as both a speaker and an attendee. That simple cross-promotion goes a long way and has led to repeat speaking invites.

  After the event, block time to review your recording. Note timestamps for standout insights and audience reactions. Those moments become clips and posts that keep working long after you leave the stage.

Case in Point: One of my clients was speaking at an industry summit. We had her share a quick "can't wait to see you tomorrow" post before the event, which led several new connections to introduce themselves in the room. During her talk, we captured a fifteen-second clip of the audience laughing at her signature story; it went straight to Instagram Stories that night. Post-event, she shared a testimonial from an attendee along with a carousel of her top three slides. The result? Not just applause in the room, but two new business inquiries that same week.

When you zoom out, this pre-, during-, and post-flow is just another repurposing lens. One talk, three phases, endless ways to keep your authority growing long after the stage lights dim.

Hidden Content = Visibility Machine

Now for the kicker: You're probably sitting on a treasure chest of hidden content: old slide decks, talk transcripts, podcast guest spots, audience feedback forms, and emails you sent that one time at 2:00 a.m.

Here's a quick exercise:

1. Pull your last three talks
2. Extract ten quotes
3. Drop them into a spreadsheet
4. Apply the One-Page, One-Liner, One Story framework (see above)
5. Voilà: ten posts, ready to go

It's not about creating more. It's about finding what you already have and putting it to work.

AI: YOUR SOUS CHEF OF CONTENT CREATION

Let me tell you a quick story to explain how I think about AI and content creation.

Imagine you're hosting a dinner party. You have a vision for the vibe: elegant yet fun, reflecting your personality. You bring in a sous chef—super talented, lightning-fast, knows every recipe ever written.

You say, "Make something impressive."

They whip up a beautiful dish. But it's not quite you. It's too formal. The spice is off. And somehow, they missed the fact you're hosting vegans.

That's what happens when you open ChatGPT and just say: "Write a LinkedIn post."

Now imagine you tell that same sous chef: "My guests are vegan and love bold flavors."

"I'm known for being quirky, not stiff."

"Here's a recipe that is always a hit with my guests."

"I once made a chili so spicy it went viral on TikTok; let's nod to that."

Suddenly, the chef gets it. They're not guessing anymore. They're amplifying your brilliance.

AI is the same. It's brilliant at helping you execute, but only when you give it your insight. AI has to work as your content intern, sounding like you or your brand, thinking like you, and scaling what already works well.

We feed it quality ingredients that make it easy and predictable to get the output and outcome you desire.

Quality Ingredients List:

- Top performing blog posts
- Top-requested presentations
- Content from your most opened email newsletters
- Best social media posts

You get it.

In just scratching the surface, here's what AI can do for you from a repurposing angle:

- Slice transcripts into captions
- Suggest new angles for one story
- Reformat a blog into a LinkedIn post
- Brainstorm hooks when your brain is fried

Here's what AI can't do:

- Be you ← This part!
- Replicate your stage presence
- Replace your voice

Think of AI as your content sous-chef. It preps the ingredients, but you're still the head chef plating the dish.

From Stage to Stream of Content

Here's the bottom line: when you walk off stage, don't walk away from your content. Repurposing is how you extend the life of your ideas, build authority between events, and turn one audience into many.

Your next talk isn't just a keynote. It's more than thirty posts, five videos, a lead magnet, and a conversation pipeline that keeps you booked and paid.

That's not extra work. That's just smart business.

So, the next time you step off stage, don't pack your brilliance away. Repurpose it. Multiply it. Let your talk keep talking for you. You never know what other invitations, inquiries, and sales opportunities will spark next.

To download your "20 Fresh Ways to Repackage Your Content Cheat Sheet," scan the QR code on the following page.

Turn One Talk Into Twenty Touchpoints

You already poured hours into that keynote.
Why let it stop there?
Download 20 Fresh Ways to Repackage Your
Content Cheat Sheet that helps speakers,
authors, and experts turn one talk into a month
of scroll-stopping posts, reels, and articles.

**KEEP YOUR STAGE MOMENTUM GOING
— LONG AFTER THE LIGHTS DIM.**

Karlyn Ankrom

Oh Snap! Social

OhSnapSocial.com

LinkedIn.com/in/karlynankrom

Instagram.com/ohsnapsocialkarlyn

Karlyn Ankrom is the founder of Oh Snap! Social and creator of the Expert Excellence Engine, a strategic content program that helps nonfiction authors turn their books from "expensive business cards" into consistent, engaging content that builds authority and drives results.

With over 20 years of experience in social media strategy and communications, Karlyn has helped hundreds of authors, speakers, and business owners make sense of social media through practical systems, clear storytelling, and strategies that actually stick. Her signature framework helps experts show up online with clarity, confidence, and consistency—without burning out.

In *Speak Your Way to Sales*, Karlyn's chapter, "Repurpose to Sell – Turning Every Talk into a Content Engine," teaches how to turn every podcast interview, keynote, or panel into content that keeps working long after the mic drops.

When she's not deep in the social media trenches, Karlyn is teaching dance, keeping up with her daughter, or sneaking away for iced coffee and breakfast sammies with her husband.

Education, Certifications, & Accreditations

- Instructor for American Marketing Association
- B.A. Journalism, James Madison University

7

DELEGATE LIKE A SPEAKER: HOW A VIRTUAL ASSISTANT EXPANDS YOUR STAGE
BY JENNIFER CRAWFORD

INTRODUCTION

You can be the most dynamic speaker on stage—captivating, insightful, unforgettable—but if your follow-up is messy, or your responses are slow, event planners will quietly move on to the next name on their list. And if you *are* booked, but you don't have time to co-promote or leverage your speaking into marketing assets, your reputation and value as a speaker will be diminished, and you won't get the full value from the opportunity.

Building your reputation as a powerful speaker takes more than showing up and delivering a great talk. Speakers who get rebooked aren't just talented; they're *organized* and *easy to work with*. They make a great impression not only with their message but also with how smoothly everything runs before and after the event. This means being a *reliable event partner* by meeting deadlines, providing polished materials, and participating in promotion. Co-promoting before, during, and after an event doesn't just raise visibility; it strengthens credibility with organizers and audiences alike.

That's where the support of a virtual assistant (VA) can make all the difference. Working with a VA will elevate you to a polished, professional, in-demand speaker by being the wizard behind the scenes, making you look good.

A skilled VA keeps your speaking business running like a professional operation—tracking outreach, confirming logistics, sending materials, and following up while you focus on preparing for the spotlight. When event organizers see that you're dependable, responsive, and professional, they don't just book you once; they remember you for future events and recommend you to others.

Each speaking engagement is also a chance to create lasting content—recordings, articles, or social posts that extend your reach long after you leave the stage. But managing all those moving parts takes time, and time is the one thing most speakers don't have enough of. That's why a virtual assistant is so valuable—someone who handles logistics, manages communications, and keeps your business running so you can focus on what you do best: delivering impact and leaving a lasting impression.

My goal in this chapter is simple: to show you how a virtual assistant (VA) can take the heavy lifting off your plate so you can focus on what really matters—showing up, speaking, and maximizing your stage time. When you delegate the right parts of the process, you don't just reduce overwhelm; you set yourself up to secure more opportunities and make every one count.

As someone who has booked speakers and owns two VA agencies, I can tell you two things with certainty: speakers who work with virtual assistants come across as far more professional and easier to partner with—and there's a *lot* more behind being a high-demand speaker than just the time on stage.

For many people, the idea of bringing on a VA to help (or anyone that needs to be delegated to) creates as much anxiety as the idea of managing speaking gigs on your own. And that's a place where I see many talented professionals get stuck—fearing to dive into something that will be big and a little overwhelming at times, but that will also have a highly beneficial impact on their business. And here is the good news: jumping into the world of delegation will eliminate almost all the anxiety of jumping into the world of speaking gigs. So, it's basically a BOGO deal: buy one VA and learn to delegate *and* build a powerful speaking pipeline at the same time.

Delegation is how you keep the spotlight where it belongs—on you—while your VA runs the systems behind the scenes. The difference between spinning your wheels and building a true speaking pipeline often comes down to how you set your VA up for success. Give them a clear process, and they'll run with it—scouting, tracking, and following up—while you stay in the spotlight delivering your message.

In this chapter, we'll guide you step by step through how to:

- Select and properly onboard a VA

- Use your VA to research and apply for speaking opportunities

- Stay organized and manage incoming opportunities without drowning in details

- Leverage each gig to grow your business and secure the next one

By the end, you'll have a simple plan for building a consistent speaking strategy—without burning yourself out.

Selecting Your VA

Before you can successfully delegate the work of building a speaking pipeline, you need the right person in the role. Not every virtual assistant will be a fit for this type of work. Securing and managing speaking opportunities requires a specific mix of skills, and taking the time to choose carefully will pay off in the quality of the results you get.

At the top of the list is **attention to detail.** A missed email, overlooked deadline, or incomplete application can mean the difference between landing a high-profile opportunity and losing it to someone else. Your VA needs to be someone who takes deadlines seriously, double-checks their work, and keeps track of multiple moving parts without letting anything slip through the cracks. **Strong writing skills** are equally important. They'll often be the ones communicating on your behalf—submitting proposals, drafting emails to event organizers, and crafting follow-ups—so their writing should reflect a professional, polished version of your voice.

A sense of **professional presentation** is another must. Your VA will often serve as the "face" of your brand in initial interactions, and how they communicate sets the tone for how organizers perceive you. A baseline familiarity with tools like **Canva** is also essential, since they may be creating or updating speaker sheets, media kits, and social media graphics. If they have some design talent or marketing experience, that's even better; it allows them to elevate the materials you use to pitch yourself and makes the entire process more effective.

Finally, **availability and responsiveness** matter more than most people realize. A VA who only checks in for a few hours once a week may be too slow to respond to inquiries or follow up with opportunities, costing you speaking engagements before you even know they existed. Ideally, your VA should be available several times throughout the week, so communication stays timely and opportunities don't fall through the cracks. If your budget allows for at least five hours a week, look for someone who can spread those hours over at least two or three days (and ideally five). Speaking opportunities often move quickly, and a VA who is present and engaged in real time will help you capture them.

Onboarding Your VA

Once you've found the right VA, don't make the mistake of throwing them into the deep end and expecting immediate perfection. Even the most skilled, proactive VA needs time to learn your preferences, brand, and workflow. Onboarding is less about handing off tasks and more about setting the relationship up for long-term success.

Start by approaching the relationship with the right **mindset.** Your VA is not just an extra set of hands; they're a partner in your speaking strategy. The more context and communication you provide, the better they can anticipate your needs and make smart decisions on your behalf. Share your goals for speaking engagements: What types of audiences are you trying to reach? What topics do you most want to be known for? How do you define a "successful" speaking opportunity? This context helps them make better choices when vetting opportunities and crafting outreach messages.

Next, invest a little time in building a shared **structure.** Walk your VA through your existing systems and workflows (or build them together if none exist yet). Show them how you like your calendar organized, how you prefer to receive updates, and where they should store research and collateral. Discuss communication expectations: how often you want check-ins, how quickly you expect them to respond to new leads, and which decisions they should run by you versus handling on their own.

It's also important to remember that **your VA can't read your mind.** The more you communicate—especially in the first few weeks—the faster they'll learn your preferences and the sooner they can start operating independently. If something isn't quite right, don't be afraid to offer feedback. And if they do something well, point it out so they know they're on the right track.

Treating onboarding as an intentional process rather than an afterthought transforms the working relationship. Instead of simply completing tasks, your VA will start thinking strategically, spotting opportunities, and proactively managing your speaking pipeline. And when that happens, the process becomes not just easier—but significantly more effective.

Becoming a Speaker: Research and Outreach Made Simple

The first step in landing speaking gigs is identifying where you want to speak. Sounds simple, right? But once you start digging, you'll realize just how many opportunities exist: podcasts, conferences, workshops, webinars, industry panels, festivals, and more. Without a system, it's easy to get lost in the noise.

This is where your VA becomes invaluable. Instead of you spending hours combing through Google searches and LinkedIn posts, your

VA can create and manage a spreadsheet to keep everything organized. I recommend that you identify what you want in the spreadsheet, communicate that to your VA, and then let her handle creating it.

Setting up your Speaking Opportunities Spreadsheet:

1. **Define Your Parameters:** Start by making rules for what you *will* and *won't* do. Maybe you only want podcasts with an audience that is exactly your ideal client niche. Maybe you'll travel up to two hours by car, but you won't fly. Maybe festivals aren't your thing. Whatever the boundaries, spell them out clearly at the top of the spreadsheet, so your VA can filter opportunities for you.

2. **Set Up Tabs by Category:** Have your VA create separate tabs for different types of opportunities, such as podcasts, conferences, membership associations, speaker bureaus, etc.

3. **Decide on Columns:** Your VA can build columns for event name, website, point of contact, application process, audience size, travel distance, and deadlines.

4. **Let Them Research:** Once the framework is in place, your VA starts filling it with real opportunities. Within days, you'll have a curated list of events that fit *your* criteria, instead of wasting time sifting through everything.

Once the first round of research is complete, your only job is to review. You'll review the spreadsheet, confirm which opportunities feel like a good fit, and then give your VA the green light to move forward.

Pro Tip: Don't skip this review step. Even with clear parameters, only *you* know which opportunities truly align with your goals and brand.

After your approval, your VA can handle the outreach: submitting applications, emailing organizers, or filling out interest forms. This alone can save you countless hours.

BUILDING YOUR SPEAKER TOOLKIT

As your VA begins outreach, you'll quickly discover that event organizers ask for a few standard materials:

- A professional bio
- A headshot
- A speaker sheet (sometimes called a media sheet or a one sheet) with your topics, past speaking experience, testimonials, books you've written or contributed to, etc.

Pro Tip: Your VA can find media sheet/one-sheet templates in Canva, which will save her a lot of time on formatting and design.

Your VA can help hold you accountable for the pieces you need to create personally, like your bio and headshot, and then take on the rest. They can draft the speaker sheet, format it beautifully, and keep it up to date as you book more gigs.

They can also manage memberships with professional organizations or speaker bureaus. Many of these groups require fees or an application process, so your VA can gather the details, present you with options, and even walk you through onboarding if you choose to join.

MANAGING YOUR SPEAKING ENGAGEMENTS

Congratulations! You have opportunities coming in. Now the challenge becomes keeping everything organized. Without a system, you risk missing deadlines, showing up unprepared, or double-booking yourself.

Your VA can step in as your central hub. Here's how:

- **Calendar Management:** When a speaking engagement is confirmed, your VA adds it to your calendar along with all key details: who's hosting, the audience, the format, deadlines, and links.

- **Preparation Summaries:** Instead of you digging through multiple emails, your VA can create a one-page overview for each event with the essential "who, what, where, when, why," and add the link to the calendar appointment or wherever it's easiest for you to access.

- **Travel Coordination:** If travel is required, your VA can book flights, hotels, and ground transportation within your parameters.

- **Ongoing Communication:** Your VA can manage emails with event organizers to ensure nothing falls through the cracks.

The result? You show up prepared and confident without spending hours in the weeds.

LEVERAGING SPEAKING GIGS FOR MAXIMUM IMPACT

Landing the gig is just the beginning. The real power of speaking comes from how you leverage each opportunity afterward. Here's where your VA shines again:

- **Promotion Beforehand:** Your VA can create and schedule social media posts, email announcements, or blog updates to let your audience know where you'll be speaking. This builds buzz and credibility.

- **Content Repurposing:** After the event, your VA can track down recordings, photos, or quotes and repurpose them into blog posts, social media clips, or additions to your speaker sheet.

- **Follow-Up:** Your VA can send thank-you notes to organizers, request testimonials, and capture audience feedback.

- **Offer Coordination:** If you made a special offer during your talk, like a free download or discounted service, your VA ensures the offer is delivered smoothly and that new leads are added to your system.

When managed well, each speaking engagement becomes a building block for the next one. Over time, you'll have a library of collateral, testimonials, and recordings that make it easier to secure bigger and better gigs.

CONCLUSION

Launching or upleveling a speaking strategy takes work, but you don't have to do it all yourself. With the right VA, even a few hours a week can move you from "overwhelmed and stuck" to "organized and consistently booking gigs."

And here's the secret: once you start delegating, you'll want to delegate more. As your VA learns your style and preferences, they'll anticipate your needs, streamline processes, and free up more of your time.

If you've never worked with a VA before, or if you've had less-than-great experiences in the past, I recommend working with an agency. Yes, it may cost a little more per hour, but the benefit is huge: you don't have to waste time finding, vetting, and training someone from scratch. At Sparent, we focus on matching you not just on skills but also on personality, so you end up with someone who truly fits your work style.

Your next step? Put a plan in place. Download our free resource, "Delegate Your Way to Speaking Gigs," which includes templates, scripts, and a roadmap for everything we covered here. Then, when you're ready, reach out. We'd love to see if we have a VA who's the right fit to help you bring your speaking strategy to life.

Imagine a speaking strategy that runs even while you're off the clock.

No more missed opportunities.

No more overwhelmed late-night research sessions.

No more feeling like you "should" be doing more to get your message out.

That system is absolutely possible — and you don't have to build it yourself.

Download Your Free Resource:

Delegate Your Way to Speaking Gigs

A practical, done-for-you guide that includes:

- Templates
- Scripts
- Checklists
- And More!

Your voice deserves a bigger platform.

Let a VA help you get there — without burning yourself out.

Jennifer Crawford

Co-CEO, Sparent, LLC
Co-CEO, Move Forward
Virtual Assistants, LLC

sparent.co
moveforwardvirtualassistants.com

@sparentco
@moveforwardvas

Jennifer Crawford is the co-founder and co-CEO of two virtual assistant agencies. In 2018, she and business partner Meredith Eaton, co-founded Sparent, where she manages a talent pool of stay-at-home moms who help overwhelmed business owners get things accomplished. In 2022, Jennifer and Meredith bought Move Forward Virtual Assistants which specializes in the administrative support of over 100 mental health practices.

With over 30 years of experience in growing service-based businesses, Jennifer has built multiple seven-figure companies and understands how important delegation and superior support are to any business's success.

In *Speak Your Way to Sales*, Jennifer shares how delegating to a virtual assistant can take you from a great speaker to an in-demand speaking professional.

In addition to running two virtual assistant agencies, Jennifer enjoys spending time in the Blue Ridge Mountains, road trips, reading, hiking, and improv.

Education, Certifications, & Accreditations
- Founded DC PodFest in 2015, the only podcasting conference in the DC Metro Area, and booked speakers nationally.
- Has helped hundreds of business owners and speakers work with virtual assistants to get the most out of their speaking opportunities.

8

STOP CHASING GIGS: BUILD YOUR BOOKING PIPELINE
BY MARY SUE DAHILL

INTRODUCTION

Early in my business, I quickly realized that speaking was one of the fastest ways to do two things: share my message with a large audience and build instant trust. I had seen the power of this model at events, conferences, and webinars, and I thought, *I can do that, too.* After all, I'd spoken plenty of times in the corporate world.

So, I wrote my talk and started looking for gigs. And wow—was I in for a surprise. Landing speaking opportunities was *work.* On top of serving clients, I was trying to keep my calendar full of speaking gigs, but I had no system for finding opportunities, tracking applications, or following up with planners. That first year, I landed only a couple of gigs.

Everything changed once I built a system. By keeping track of where I applied, consistently following up, and treating speaking like a process—not a one-off hustle—I booked far more gigs in my second year.

Here's the truth: great talks and good intentions don't automatically translate into speaker bookings. Without a system, you miss application windows, slip off a planner's radar, or lose the chance to be in the right place at the right time.

And part of what holds speakers back is the myths we tell ourselves. Let's set the record straight:

- **Myth:** *If I'm good enough, event planners will find me.*
  Truth: Great talks don't magically generate bookings. You have to put yourself out there consistently.
- **Myth:** *One perfect pitch is all it takes.*
  Truth: Organizers get hundreds of submissions. Follow-up is what gets you remembered.
- **Myth:** *Paid speaking is only for celebrities or big names.*
  Truth: Businesses like yours can and do get paid for speaking; it comes down to positioning, persistence, and a system.
- **Myth:** *Referrals will keep my calendar full.*
  Truth: Referrals are wonderful, but they're unpredictable. A pipeline gives you control.

You don't need luck or celebrity status. You need a simple, consistent system.

In this chapter, I'll show you how to transform your speaking outreach into a *booking pipeline*—one that consistently fills your calendar with opportunities and turns every stage into momentum for your business.

However, before we dig into the system itself, let's look at the outreach problem no one talks about—the real reason so many great speakers still struggle to get booked.

THE OUTREACH PROBLEM NO ONE TALKS ABOUT

Speaking is one of the fastest ways to build trust and authority—but here's the problem no one talks about: *having a brilliant talk doesn't guarantee you'll get booked.* Speaking as a growth strategy isn't a secret; it's one of the most popular ways to market a business, which means you're competing with dozens, sometimes hundreds, of other talented speakers all vying for the same stage. Event planners are overwhelmed with options. The real challenge isn't your talk; it's your outreach.

Most speakers don't struggle because they lack talent. They struggle because their outreach is inconsistent. They send one pitch and never follow up. They scatter applications across email folders and sticky notes, then forget where they applied. They treat every gig as a lucky break rather than as part of a predictable system. And that's why their calendars stay half-empty.

The solution is probably easier than you think. You don't have to be the most creative; you just have to be the most consistent. When you have a strong system that facilitates steady follow-up and a repeatable process, you'll easily outpace most speakers.

OUTREACH TRAPS TO AVOID

- **Pitch Once, Then Vanish:** Silence rarely means "no." It usually means the planner is busy and needs a reminder.

- **Losing Track of Outreach:** If you don't know where you applied, you can't follow up—and missed follow-ups = missed gigs.

- **Treating Gigs Like Lucky Breaks:** Speaking is a numbers game: consistent outreach leads to predictable bookings.

- **Waiting on Referrals:** Referrals are wonderful, but they're unpredictable. A pipeline gives you control.

"Luck is what happens when preparation meets opportunity."
—*Seneca*

Here's the truth:

- **Preparation** = skills, systems, and follow-through
- **Opportunity** = the open door, the call for speakers, the planner's inbox

- **Luck** = when you've already done the work and are ready to step in

Don't wait for luck. Build your system. Create your own opportunities. That's how you stop chasing gigs and start getting booked.

The best part is that it doesn't have to be complicated. With the right *booking pipeline,* you can organize every opportunity, track your outreach, and follow up with confidence.

Let's break down exactly how that works.

The Framework for Your Booking Pipeline

If outreach is the problem, your *booking pipeline* is the solution. Think of it as the GPS for your speaking business; it gives you visibility, keeps you on course, and helps you reach your destination without missing critical turns.

A booking pipeline is simply a visual map of the stages a speaking opportunity goes through, from the moment you spot a lead to the moment you're officially booked. Its purpose is to organize, track, and manage your outreach so nothing slips through the cracks.

Here's what makes a pipeline powerful:

- **Visibility:** See exactly where every opportunity stands
- **Focus:** Know what needs attention today
- **Consistency:** Follow a repeatable process instead of starting from scratch
- **Tracking:** Spot patterns, improve conversion rates, and scale what works

Instead of relying on luck or scattered notes, you'll have a system that moves opportunities forward one stage at a time.

Step 1: Create Your Pipeline in a CRM

Here's the simple structure I recommend:

Lead → Outreach (Application/Pitch) → Follow-Up → Call → Negotiation → Agreement → Booked

- **Lead:** A potential opportunity—referral, listing, or intro.
- **Outreach:** Submit your pitch or application and log what you sent.
- **Follow-Up:** Nurture the relationship with reminders, nudges, or encouragement.
- **Call:** If a planner books a call, you're on the shortlist—capture needs and decision dates.
- **Negotiation:** Align scope, format, and compensation (fee, books, list access, or hybrid).
- **Agreement:** Proposal/contract/payment link sent. This signals intent.
- **Booked:** Signed, paid, or accepted. Add to your calendar with deliverables and travel.

Outreach and follow-up may sound similar, but they're different. Outreach is your initial ask. Follow-up is how you keep the conversation alive once interest is shown.

Step 2: Capture Every Opportunity

This is the habit that changes everything. Early on, I made the mistake of applying and never recording it. Once, I even won a gig but missed it because I didn't log it. Painful.

Don't let that happen to you. Capture details like:

- Event title + link
- Date, time, and location

- Application open/close dates + link
- Audience description and purpose
- Why you're a fit (short summary)
- Organizer contact info + social links

Log this immediately into your CRM. Dates trigger reminders, and tentative gigs on a "speaking calendar" give you a clear view of what's ahead.

Step 3: Outreach (Application/Pitch)

Apply or pitch, then record what you submitted and the decision timeline. Tailor your talk title and outcomes to align with the event's goals. Your positioning makes you stand out.

Step 4: Follow-Up

This is where most speakers fall off. Don't just ask, "Did you get my application?" Build a relationship:

- Connect with organizers on LinkedIn
- Engage meaningfully with event posts
- Check in around decision dates
- Stay on the radar for recurring events

If it feels like a lot, a trained VA can handle much of it. The key is consistency.

Step 5: Call

If a planner schedules a call, you've moved into serious consideration. Treat it like a discovery call: clarify needs, confirm decision dates, and log everything in your CRM.

Step 6: Negotiation

Decide upfront what types of compensation work for you: keynote fees, breakout sessions, books, lists, or hybrids. Keep momentum alive with reminders so you don't lose ground during back-and-forth.

Step 7: Agreement → Booked

Speed matters. Use ready-to-go agreement templates, e-signature, and payment tools to close quickly. Once booked, add everything—dates, deliverables, travel—to your calendar or project tool so nothing slips through the cracks.

Why Not Just Use a Spreadsheet?

A spreadsheet can hold information, but it can't send reminders, automate follow-ups, or manage agreements. A CRM pipeline transforms chaos into clarity.

Now here's the real magic: once you have a pipeline, you can start to see patterns in your outreach. That's where consistency and numbers come in—and why *the math behind consistency* is the key to turning effort into predictable bookings.

The Math Behind Consistency

Consistency is the secret weapon in booking speaking gigs because, at the end of the day, it's a numbers game. Yes, you can have a fantastic talk and pitch to the right audiences, but so much of the decision-making process is out of your hands. That's why you can't pin all your hopes on a few "perfect" opportunities. You need to consistently throw your hat in the ring for many good opportunities.

Here's the part most speakers miss: booking gigs works just like sales. To succeed, you have to consistently pitch and apply, nurture relationships, follow up, track your results, and look for patterns.

For example:

- You might discover that for every *ten applications,* you land *two gigs.*
- That means if your goal is *twelve gigs a year,* you'll need to apply for about *sixty opportunities.*
- You may also find that certain talk titles or topics resonate better with event planners than others.

Without a system, this math is invisible. With a pipeline, you can see exactly how your activity translates into results. That turns speaking from a hopeful hustle into a *repeatable process.*

And here's the best part: once you know what's working, you can build on it. Building doesn't just mean sending more pitches; it could mean:

- Hiring a virtual assistant to scale your outreach
- Targeting bigger events with larger audiences
- Expanding the types of speaking opportunities you pursue
- Traveling with confidence because you know the return will be worth it

Consistency gives you power. When you track and measure your outreach, you can predict how many gigs you'll land, evaluate whether they're profitable, and make speaking a reliable growth engine for your business.

A BEFORE-AND-AFTER SNAPSHOT

I've worked with several speakers who generated most of their business through speaking engagements. Let's look at the example of "Sophia", who represents most of my speaking clients. Sophia didn't charge for her speaking because she would make an offer as part of her presentation or workshop. Speaking was incredibly important to

Sophia's business because she would get a handful of prospects from each engagement, which would turn into a couple of clients. They were incredibly profitable for her business. Sophia reached out to me for help because she didn't have a system for securing speaking gigs, and she had done the rounds among her friends and business peers. The typical places she had been speaking were drying up, and she needed to expand her circle of influence, which meant organizing how she managed her outreach.

Sophia was largely managing her speaker opportunities in email folders or a half-filled-out spreadsheet. She would do a little research, fill out some applications, then cross her fingers and hope she was selected. She often forgot where she applied, so she didn't know who to follow up with and missed several opportunities.

Sophia was attracted to the Revenue Accelerator for Speakers because it wasn't just a CRM; it had a system built for what she needed, along with training to help her use it. She knew that if she purchased a different system, she would have to spend countless hours defining her system and watching videos to make it work for her. Those were hours that she needed to spend on existing clients, researching speaking gigs, or simply enjoying her life.

After completing our VIP Day, during which she learned how to set up the Revenue Accelerator for Speakers, Sophia had all her speaking gig opportunities in the pipeline. She was ready to start following up the next day. She loved having a set of email templates that she could easily pull from to use in her outreach that were professional and easily customized to her business. Sophia appreciated the small-group training to ensure she could use the tools and stay on top of her speaking leads.

Sophia felt like she was no longer chaotically chasing opportunities. She finally had a system, so she consistently followed up on every lead and didn't leave any speaking opportunities on the table.

That meant Sophia needed to apply to many more speaking opportunities than she had been to close the number of gigs she needed to hit her revenue goals. With that knowledge, she engaged a virtual assistant to assist her with research, outreach, follow-up, and scheduling. After being in the program for six months, Sophia doubled the number of gigs she closed compared to the previous six months and was booking into the following year.

Having a speaker pipeline, system, and software made managing the entire process easier and helped Sophia book more speaking gigs. Speaking gigs were Sophia's preferred engine for business growth. She shifted speaking from a chance booking to a scalable system.

If you are like Sophia and serious about landing speaking gigs without the chaos, you need a system.

Step Into the Revenue Accelerator for Speakers

There's no shortage of CRMs and software tools out there. You probably own a few already. The problem is that they all require you to *define your system, build it from scratch, and figure out how to use it.* That takes time, energy, and—if you hire help—money.

After working with countless speakers who are also business owners, I realized they didn't need another blank software tool. They needed a *ready-to-use system* designed specifically for how speakers book gigs. That's why I created the Revenue Accelerator for Speakers.

This isn't just software; it's a complete *speaker booking pipeline* that mirrors the exact stages we've covered in this chapter. Inside, you'll find:

- A pre-built pipeline for managing speaking opportunities
- Over twenty customizable email templates to streamline outreach and follow-up
- Task automations and optional email automations that keep opportunities moving forward
- A simple dashboard for tracking progress and results at a glance
- VIP Day onboarding + small-group training, so you can use it effectively from day one

I've seen too many business owners spend thousands on software that ends up sitting unused because they never had the time or technical know-how to set it up. The Revenue Accelerator for Speakers eliminates that problem. It's already built with everything speakers need, so you can skip the guesswork and focus on what matters: *landing more gigs that bring in paying clients or paid speaking fees.*

Best of all, it's *customizable where it counts.* You can tweak the email templates to match your voice, topics, and brand—but fewer than 10 percent of my clients ever change the actual pipeline. Why? Because it's simple, effective, and works—right out of the box.

Picture This...

Imagine opening your CRM and seeing thirty speaking opportunities in progress. You know exactly which planners you've pitched, which ones need follow-up, and which are close to being booked.

Imagine having reminders built in so you never wonder, *Who should I reach out to today?* Instead, you start every week with clarity and confidence.

Imagine booking next year's calendar before this year is over because you have a predictable process that turns applications into confirmed gigs.

That's what happens when you stop chasing gigs in chaos and start running your speaking outreach like a system.

If this sounds like the system you've been missing, *scan the QR code and book a call to see how the Revenue Accelerator for Speakers can transform your speaking business.*

Wrap-Up

If you use speaking to grow your business or you're building a career as a paid speaker, it's time to stop chasing gigs with chaos and start booking them with confidence.

Throughout this chapter, you've seen why speaking builds authority and trust, but also why so many opportunities slip away: no system, no follow-up, and no consistency. You've also learned the simple framework for building a *speaker booking pipeline.* This structure helps you capture every opportunity, track every outreach, follow up with purpose, and ultimately close more gigs.

Success on stage doesn't start when you grab the microphone; it starts the moment you treat speaking like a repeatable business process. With a clear pipeline, you'll know exactly where each opportunity stands, when to follow up, and how to turn applications into booked stages. That means more predictability in your calendar, more consistency in your revenue, and more freedom to focus on delivering great talks.

Whether you're aiming for paying clients through lead-generating talks or building a steady flow of paid engagements, the path forward is the same: *a simple, consistent system that ensures no opportunity is left behind.*

It's time to move from scattered efforts to a streamlined process. From hoping to be chosen to creating your momentum. From chasing gigs to being booked solid.

With the right speaker booking pipeline, every lead becomes a revenue opportunity, every follow-up a step closer to the stage, and every stage an engine for growth in your business.

Scan the QR Code for your free checklist and special offers for the Revenue Accelerator for Speakers.

This Is Exactly How You Get More Booked Gigs!

Scan the QR Code to access:

☑ Your free Speaker's Booking Pipeline Toolkit

☑ Special offers for the Revenue Accelerator for Speakers

Stop chasing gigs. Start booking them—with confidence, consistency, and a system that works.

Mary Sue Dahill

Work Smarter Digital

www.worksmarterdigital.com

@worksmarterdigital

@marysuedahill

Mary Sue Dahill is the founder and CEO of Work Smarter Digital, helping service-based founders streamline operations, integrate AI, and scale profitably with smart CRM systems and automation. With more than 25 years in technology, startups, and business management, she has guided hundreds of entrepreneurs in building sales systems that turn chaos into consistent, scalable revenue. She is a HighLevel Certified Admin and the author of The Boutique Effect and The Solopreneur's Dilemma.

In *Speak Your Way to Sales*, Mary Sue led the book's development and contributes a chapter on how speakers can stop chasing gigs and start booking them with confidence using her Revenue Accelerator for Speakers—a practical system for organizing outreach, tracking opportunities, and landing more paid and referral-driving engagements.

Outside of work, Mary Sue enjoys slow mornings with her husband and two mini dachshunds, sipping coffee on the patio, and planning travel adventures from her home in Arlington, Virginia.

Education, Certifications, & Accreditations

- Master of Science in Management of Information Technology, University of Virginia
- Certified HighLevel Admin, HighLevel (2024)

9

THE REAL POWER OF THE STAGE: GENERATING REVENUE!
BY KATIE NELSON

I was approached to write this chapter of *Speak Your Way to Sales* very explicitly, specifically because, as a business coach, I focus on the top and bottom line. More specifically, I work with my clients to create a focus around the revenue they want, the money they want to make, and the growth that can be had by paying attention to and intentionally focusing on how to generate income for themselves and their businesses.

For over nine years, I have taught my clients how speaking is *absolutely* a revenue stream if they are intentional about it. (And I am not just talking about speaker fees, but we'll get to that in a minute.) I've even done a "big stage," where I hosted a two-day live event on this *exact topic.* I am very passionate about generating revenue through stages because it is such a powerful tool for solopreneurs and microbusinesses who want to grow revenue as easily as possible.

The goal of my chapter is to impart the mindset, strategy, and system to turn your speaking into a repeatable revenue engine you can use for business expansion now and later.

So, let's get to it, shall we? Marketing is the easy go-to for being on stages, being seen, growing market share, and showing your expertise. Wonderful! Now on to how to *monetize* it all. We'll go over six easy-to-remember steps, and I want you to take what you need for where you are in your business and make it work for you (read: make money/generate revenue) every step of the way.

STEP 1: IT ALL STARTS WITH MINDSET

If you started your business so that your only job was to be a professional speaker, this chapter may not be for you. The path to that cash and growth for your business looks very different from that of most service-based businesses. For those of you who have an expertise outside of speaking and presenting that you use to generate your revenue, this is where it starts. The mindset to have is that speaking on stages isn't just a performance or a way to get your name out there, but it is 100 percent a business development system. As you speak on stages, the goal, of course, is to educate, engage, and even entertain. The goal of this mindset shift is that you realize it is even better for moving the right prospects closer to the yes—to doing business with you.

In shifting your mindset, there are key questions to ask yourself to prepare for the right stages. (If you're reading this and you know me, try not to roll your eyes, please.)

1. Is my target audience here? As we know, the "riches are in the niches." Are you speaking to a room filled with your niche?

2. Is this speaking engagement a front-end (speaker fee) or back-end (call to action) engagement?

3. What are my goals for this engagement? For example, if it's marketing, how much more reach do you receive? If it's business development, what is your goal for referrals, clients, or revenue (aka $$$)?

Once you create this mindset shift, you are now thinking like a CEO or business owner. The stage and your talk become less about performance and more about providing potential clients with a reason to say yes to you. You are showing them, in every way possible, why you are the right choice to solve their problems.

Step 2: Strategic Stage Selection

Now that you have your mindset fully focused on revenue generation, this one should be a little easier. After all, not all stages have the same purpose for your business. As mentioned previously, if you are looking at the marketing side of the house, you'll ask different filtering questions. The focus here is on growing your client list and your bank account.

Filtering questions:

1. **Audience Match:** Is this room filled to the brim with my target audience? Is this room filled with the people who have the problems I solve and have the budget to afford my services? Is this room worth my time if I am focused on growing my revenue, and it doesn't have these qualifications?

2. **Content Fit:** This is closely related to audience match (aka the "square peg, round hole" question). Can your message be tailored so that the audience clearly and concisely understands what you do? Are you trying to make your content fit into an audience that hasn't proven to be buyers? So tricky, right? It is so easy for us to say, "Yes, I should be in this room, regardless." As entrepreneurs, our hopefulness can work against us sometimes, leading us to make an argument for every yes. Is that the right thing for our goals, though? How much time does it take you to provide an amazing experience from the stage? Is there enough potential in that room to even cover your hard and soft costs, like your time? If the answer is yes, this stage gets filtered into your schedule, *wahoo!* Now, go get new clients.

3. **Revenue Potential:** This differs slightly from audience match, where we ask whether our buying clients are in the room. How many ways does this stage provide us with revenue potential? We know we shouldn't (really) be making a move in our business unless we have the opportunity to monetize it. (It's a slippery slope to non-profitability if we do.) The

questions for this include: Does this stage pay my fee up front to cover all my costs, so even if I don't gain a single client, I won't lose money? How many ways can I monetize this stage? Will they let me market to their list? (Remember that this is a slow way to create know, like, and trust.) Will they let me have a call to action that lets the audience voluntarily sign up for my list (a faster way to monetize)? The prioritization of stages with the greatest revenue potential is key.

Ultimately, if your stage doesn't check at least two of these three boxes, deprioritize the opportunity until it is a fit for you and your business. If that feels antithetical to your growth, I understand, but it isn't. Our focus on intentionality and growth depends on our ability to say no so we can say yes to what fits us and our goals.

STEP 3*: CREATING A TALK THAT SELLS

***This is the next step if you already have your back-end offer. If not, reverse steps 3 and 4.**

How many times have you been to a workshop, for example, where you heard the best information? The speaker gave you insight and maybe a strategy into the exact thing you needed answers for, and you knew they were the ones you wanted to work with. Then—*wah wah*—after the Q&A, on their very last slide, they gave you one minute to grab their QR code, "If you want to connect further." Or worse, they let you know that there is a special on a class they're giving with a discount, but they rushed through the offer and got off stage, leaving you to chase them down for the next bit of info. Or what about the reverse, watching those on the stage come at you with an offer after *every* slide? Or when they are teaching you from a stage, but all you hear is that you won't get this one thing right until you work with them, and the talk left you feeling deflated, even though, technically, they have let you know how to fix it all—for a fee.

Neither of these is ideal, and yes, I know you've been in those rooms because we have all been in them. (Can I tell you a secret? I almost didn't write this chapter because of a room like that once.)

Let me give you the absolute chef's kiss of a talk structure that will never steer you wrong. This talk is perfect for priming the pump to sell to your audience. The pieces of it are simple. You've likely seen them or heard them before somewhere along the way, but maybe they haven't worked before. I'll give you the answers as to why and how to make sure that doesn't happen to you again.

For those of you who remember writing papers in school, way back in the day, we were told intro, follow-up points, and summary. Another way to say this is to first tell them what you are going to tell them. Then tell them. Then tell them what you told them.

And this structure is still the best one. Both of those hold true.

First, I will give you the *power move.* Your whole presentation should be in the language of your target market. Utilize the language that your clients use, not some industry jargon that doesn't hit them or that they don't recognize.

Intro: Open with your *"attention getter."* This can be a story, a relevant statistic, or a provocative question (my favorite), followed by the challenges or problems your target market faces.

Follow-up points: This includes the paragraphs in your paper that outline the *process* and *proof,* both of which demonstrate to your audience that you are the expert. And that is why you are on this stage. The process includes what you provide in terms of a framework, solutions to their problems, or strategies to solve their problems. Get where they are looking to go.

Throughout your intro and follow-up points, you can sprinkle your CTA (call to action). This is called seeding, and it is showing your audience that they can trust you. They will get everything they came for, and if they want more, you have them covered with your CTA.

Lastly, your summary: This is where you remind them that you understand their challenges, summarize how you support them in overcoming them, and then outline the steps forward for working with you. This is also known as your ask, your sell, or your call to action.

The key to unlocking their purchasing power is to ensure *equal time is allotted* to each section of your "paragraphs," including your ask. Your call to action is not something to rush through. When you do, you lose your audience. They feel the nervousness. They feel what you communicate, and if you are running through your offer, you are communicating nerves. If you are in any way uneasy about the call to action or about asking the audience to buy your services, you will erode all the expertise and relationships you have built over the course of your time on stage.

Remember, equal time. Relax into it. All you are doing is alighting the path forward so they can get from where they are to where they want to be. And you are letting them know that you are *exactly* the right person to get them there. So, tell them how to connect with you because they *want to know* (or at least the right ones do)!

STEP 4*: DESIGN YOUR BACK END OFFER – MONETIZE

***This is only for those who don't have a high-end offer yet.**

There are so many gains from having something for your people to do after they see you speak. And the risk of *not* having a CTA is that you're leaving an unknowable amount of money on the table. And why worry about that when you can address it up front with an offer? I didn't always understand this. Can't I just get up there, give people the "good stuff," and have a QR code tell them how to get in touch later?

I've been in sales my whole life, and I never sold from a stage until nine years ago, when I started Sales UpRising, my third business. It was such a strange concept. I was so good at collecting business cards, creating a system, and selling the "old school" way. That is, until *my* business coach (way back in the day) got me to see it in a different light.

My coach, Tommi, disliked selling like nobody's business, so we were very different in that respect. However, she had a great point— and revenue data to back it up—that if selling "isn't your jam" but you absolutely *love* providing solutions to problems, selling from the stage is the best option for you. Instead of selling to individuals, you are using that time to sell to the group. If you have your high-end offer ready to go, how many do you need to sell to hit your financial target? Instead of making hundreds of sales calls, you stand on a stage and pour your expertise into a room full of people hungry for your solution. Either way, you will get there, but which one sounds more efficient and easier? I mean, if you'll be on stages anyway, or already are on stages, let's generate some revenue!

Now, depending on where you are in your business, you may not have a high-ticket offer. For fast and efficient revenue generation, it can be the goal as you and your business grow.

If this is you and you are speaking on the stage for *marketing,* use a free lead magnet (PDF, checklist, or workbook) or a discovery call as your CTA.

If you are a little more tenured and have created packages and offerings, and since this chapter is on monetizing your time on stage, then *sell* your next workshop or training. Or if you have an online course, *sell* that. If a high-ticket offer is already on your list of available purchases, and if you've had enough time on stage to gain audience trust and buy-in, *sell* that! (Reread Step 3, if needed.)

In essence, that is how to monetize your speaking gigs *immediately,* and, of course, there is always more than one way to make money from a single opportunity.

Step 5: Squeeze All the Juice

Speaking on stage isn't an instant success kind of thing. Selling from stages isn't either. Turning stages into clients successfully, when done right, is a long game. The quick wins are nice, but we are looking for sustainability. To create that, speak more and build more momentum. This falls under the topic of easy to say, harder to do; however, it still holds true. The more you speak, the better you get. The better you get, the more opportunities to generate revenue there are. Throughout these chapters, you can see that each stage you stand on builds your brand, credibility, and your audience, which also means your bank account, when you focus on your goals. Every stage is a part of the larger strategy for your business growth, not a one-and-done. If you approach it from that angle from the start, there is a compounding effect to your work: more leads, more referrals, more clients, and, yes, more money!

STEP 6: THE BEST PART – THE DATA

Now, maybe data isn't your favorite part of your job as a business owner. I get that. I am more of a people person than a number cruncher, believe it or not. However, when my clients call to let me know that nothing is working in their business and they're failures and they just don't understand what they're doing wrong, why nothing is working (we've had those days, right?), my response is always, "Let's look at the data." I let them know that I completely understand, but please humor me, and let's look at the data. Data doesn't lie, and I cannot tell you how many times, once we dive into the data, the answers become so obvious. The reality is that they aren't failing; they are a little more tired than usual because things are working. The data and dollars are there to prove it.

All of that to say, if you want to see how well you can truly do from a stage and get compounding results, *track your metrics!* It can be as simple as you need it to be, but you will want to keep track of how many stages, the number of leads captured per stage, the conversion rate (how many sales come from how many prospects), total revenue generated per stage, etc. The list can be as long and as detailed as you want. As you become more familiar with what you can do, I encourage you to also track your referrals, including prospects from other stages and potential clients from each stage.

This data can provide you with a multitude of important answers for you and your business; the least of which is allowing you to refine the stages that are worth your time and to double your efforts to exponentially increase your income.

There are so many amazing ways to monetize any stage you're on, and I hope you never leave one without a dollar earned ever again. To make sure the deck is stacked in your favor, let's cover a couple of extra points for those who have stretch revenue goals.

EXTRA POINT 1: WORK THE ROOM

Your speaking engagement is a fraction of the dollars you could have available to you. If you are only showing up for your time on stage, you are leaving money on the table, and why do that? You've put so much time and effort into your stage time. Let's get you all the dollars possible. If you can, show up early, stay after, and create spaces in your calendar for prospect meetings while you are there. You won't be able to replicate the know, like, and trust you've created with your stage time, so get it while the getting is good (as my grandmother used to say).

During your pre-stage time, meet with the organizers. While they may not be your target audience, they know lots of people they can refer you to, including those with access to stages, so spend some time with them. You can also connect with other event organizers. If they like you, they might buy, so meet with the organizers. Let them get to know you beyond your bio. They are the people who have access to stages, so spend some time with them.

Meet with the vendors. Do you know who is always at the events? Vendors—and their companies need solutions, too.

Meet the other attendees. If you are hosting a breakout room, go meet some of the other attendees who won't have the opportunity to see what you are all about.

During the "intermissions," make yourself available to attendees who you saw resonating with your message, or to those looking to speak to you. Make sure that you have their information and listen to what they're saying. They are telling you how they like to be communicated with, and this is one of the keys to converting any prospect to a client, even if during the break is not the time to directly ask for their business.

After the stage, it may feel like you've "left it all on the stage." The more you practice, the more energy you will have for the before, during, and after portion, and when you do, you'll see your conversion rate go up (more on that in a minute). If you have energy, hang around. Members of the audience will want to speak to you; what they have to say is paramount to your current and future success. This is when you can gauge where your message did or didn't hit, and this is where there is real money to be made. Even if you made your offer as clear as possible on stage, there will always be people with questions, and you want to be available to answer them and take their credit card. The relationships that haven't converted on stage are the relationships that are built after and can have the ability to turn one stage into multiple opportunities.

EXTRA POINT 2: BE AUTHENTICALLY RELENTLESS IN YOUR FOLLOW-UP

Oh, I know, you can't believe that I'm talking about follow-up when it comes to sales, can you? Ha! Here is another way to look at it. It is not your prospect's job to chase you and have you at the top of their minds. It would be nice if they did, but it is highly unlikely. Data will give you the facts: that even the best presentation will provoke someone to follow up with us. And that's okay, we get paid to follow up on our potential. Whether it is one or five hundred audience members who opt in to your CTA or get halfway through the application but never submit their credit card information, your follow-up process is what will make or break your ability to turn that stage into more dollars than what was collected at the event itself.

GENERAL BEST PRACTICES

Urgency, get you some! *Speed matters.* Sending your follow-up within twenty-four hours may sound thirsty, and it is, to an extent, and it should be because your business *is* thirsty! Thirsty for cash flow. You don't want to lose any momentum because of a perceived "thirstiness;" you want to capitalize on the energy you expended.

If you have a system and it is possible, *segment your audience*. This way, you can personalize your messages based on their level of interest.

Add value to what you've already shared. Your expertise is deep and wide. You can't give it all away on one stage, so share more. Add a tip, a story, a resource. Continue to show why you are the right choice for them to say yes. And in case you forgot, this is where you remind them of how they can work with you; show them the offer again.

Show them the way. Close out the follow-up with the next step. Point them to booking a call. Have them watch the video, buy the course, or join a program.

While you can—and will, if you focus on it—make money from the stage. Most of the audience won't be an immediate conversion. Don't leave those dollars on the table. Keep nurturing those relationships. Consistency is key to any relationship.

I could say more, but I think you get the picture.

Speaking isn't just bright lights and the big city. It isn't just about ego and being the center of attention. If done right, it can be, as you've seen through these chapters, your marketing channel, your credibility machine, a cornerstone to your company brand, and absolutely your top sales approach force, all at the same time. Again, you're looking to turn your stages into a strategy for leveraging your impact and relationships to create more revenue.

Every acceptance of a speaking stage should be predicated on the question, "How can this stage grow my business?" You take that final answer and reverse engineer every move you make after that—from the presentation you deliver and the offer you make, to the follow-up you provide—to guarantee you will get to your final destination.

What you focus on becomes clear. What you think about, you bring about. All businesses need revenue to be successful; that is the definition of business. Once you have it down, the revenue potential is endless. How much do you want to make? Whatever it is, dream bigger, then go for it!

YOU'RE INVITED: STRAIGHT UP!

All Integrity. All Accountability. All the Time.

This is not a networking group. This is not a "learning more" club. This is an opportunity to say YES to you! It is an accountability group designed to help you stay accountable to your Speak Your Way to Sales goals.

This group will help you stay accountable to your GOALS: how many stages you book, staying on track with follow up, your pitching from stage, how much you earn from stages (front end and back end)!

Everything that has to do with Speak Your Way to Sales is how this group can support you!

Join now and get a FREE month of Straight UP!

Katie Nelson

Sales UpRising

salesuprising.com

linkedin.com/company/salesuprising

facebook.com/salesuprising

Katie Nelson is a business strategist at Sales UpRising, where she empowers solopreneurs with the tools and strategies to break into six-figure revenues.

With 30+ years of experience in sales, Katie has helped 200+ entrepreneurs, helped generate $7.59 million in revenue, and built 3 businesses. She specializes in business coaching and is an expert in sales.

In Speak Your Way To Sales, Katie shares actionable tips to help you turn speaking gigs into growth for your business.

Beyond business consulting, Katie enjoys keeping life creative with painting, doodling, reading, and connecting with people from all walks of life. She lives in Northern Virginia with her husband, Adam, and spicy fur baby, Julius.

Education, Certifications, & Accreditations

- Bachelor's of Interdisciplinary Studies, Communications & Sociology, ASU 2001
- Smart CEO, Brava Award Winner, 2015
- Washington Business Journal, Best Places to Work, 2015
- Start Up Certified
- 3x Biz Owner

Ready to Become an Author Without Writing a Whole Book?

You don't need to take on a full manuscript to make a real impact. Contributing a chapter lets you share your expertise, strengthen your authority, and reach new audiences without the pressure of producing an entire book. It's a focused, strategic way to get your ideas in print.

If you've been craving more visibility and credibility, this path keeps things doable while still delivering major results. You bring the insight, we handle the structure, editing, design, and publishing.

Why Contribute a Chapter

- Position yourself as a trusted expert in your space
- Share a story, strategy, or framework in a high-impact format
- Join a community of aligned professionals promoting together
- Add "Published Author" to your bio with far less stress
- Reach readers who are actively searching for support and solutions

Your Next Move

If authorship feels exciting but manageable, you're in the right place. **Download the Ebook: *10x Your Business with a Collaborative Book*** Inside, you'll learn how a well-crafted chapter can expand your reach, elevate your brand, and open new doors for your business, all without writing the full book yourself.

Your voice belongs on the page. Start here.

Meredith Eaton

Ceo, Eaton Press, LLC
Co-CEO, Sparent, LLC
Co-CEO, Move Forward Virtual
Assistants, LLC

EatonPress.com
sparent.co
moveforwardvirtualassistants.com
@sparentco
@moveforwardvas

Meredith Eaton is the CEO of Eaton Press, where she has spent over a decade helping business professionals turn their expertise into powerful nonfiction books. With a proven track record of guiding authors to write books that open doors to speaking engagements and fuel business growth, Meredith is passionate about transforming ideas into impact. Through her signature programs and personalized support, she empowers entrepreneurs to become published authorities in their fields.

In *Speak Your Way to Sales*, Meredith opens the book with an insightful introduction and lead the developmental editing process, ensuring every chapter reflects the author's unique voice and expertise.

Meredith is also the Co-CEO of Sparent, LLC, and Move Forward Virtual Assistants, serving businesses and mental health practices.

Beyond being a CEO, Meredith enjoys spending time with her 4 grandchildren, going to the beach as often as possible, and doing jigsaw puzzles while watching reality TV or crime shows.

Education, Certifications, & Accreditations

- Received an M.A. in Organizational Management from George Washington University
- Earned a certificate in The Psychology of Leadership from Cornell University
- Serves as a mentor for undergrad entreprenuership students

Meet the Experts Behind the Ideas

This book is built on the experience of people who don't just talk about their craft; they've mastered it. Each contributor brings a unique blend of strategy, creativity, and hard-earned lessons from the work they do every day. These are practitioners who solve real problems, guide real clients, and shape real outcomes.

In the following pages, you'll get a closer look at who they are, the expertise they're known for, and the lens they bring to their field. You'll also find simple ways to stay connected or explore their work further if their approach speaks to you.

Think of this section as your chance to meet the minds behind the material—skilled and thoughtful professionals who helped make this book not just useful but actionable.

Chapter 1: Crafting Your Personal Brand Story for the Stage by Jen Dalton

Jen Dalton

BrandMirror

www.brandmirror.com

linkedin.com/in/jennifervdalton

@jenvdalton

Jen Dalton is the CEO and founder of BrandMirror, where she specializes in personal branding strategy, working with executives, entrepreneurs, and organizations to clarify their purpose, elevate their visibility, and create lasting impact in their industries.

With over 20 years of experience in brand and business strategy, Jen has partnered with Fortune 500 companies, coached thousands of leaders, published bestselling books such as *The Intentional Entrepreneur* and *Listen*, and been recognized as an Entrepreneurial Leader of the Year at Georgetown University. She is an international speaker, author, and certified personal brand strategist who helps leaders and organizations define, deliver, and amplify their unique value and promise.

In *Speak Your Way To Sales*, Jen shares actionable strategies for leveraging your personal brand to build confidence, shape your narrative, and spark meaningful conversations that drive results. This ties the chapter's focus back to helping professionals authentically connect and convert through intentional talks and speaking engagements.

Beyond her professional focus, Jen enjoys giving back to the community through board service at organizations helping families and women leaders, living in Northern Virginia with her family, and pursuing passion projects in leadership development and storytelling.

Education, Certifications, & Accreditations

- EMBA, Georgetown University McDonough School of Business (2010–2012)
- BSBA, International Management & Human Resources, Georgetown University (1995–1999)
- Master Personal Brand Strategist & 360 Reach Analyst, Reach Personal Branding
- PROSCI Change Management Certification
- 1 Million Cups Certified Organizer (Kauffman Foundation)
- Strategies that Build Winning Brands, Kellogg School of Management (Northwestern University)

Ready to amplify your brand and impact?

Schedule a free consult with Jen Dalton today to clarify your unique value and accelerate your visibility.

Scan the QR Code to access:

- ☑ Connect on LinkedIn
- ☑ Schedule a Consult
- ☑ Download Your LinkedIn Checklist
- ☑ Download Your Personal Brand Worksheet
- ☑ and even more!!!

Telepathy is not a strategy.
Contact Jen directly at
jendalton@brandmirror.com or call 703-898-8691
for bookings, questions, or inquiries.

Chapter 2: Speaking in Stories: Turning Complex Topics Into Relatable Ideas
by Nancy D. Greene, Esq.

Nancy D. Greene, Esq.

N D Greene, PC

NGDLaw.com

linkedin.com/in/attorneynancygreene/

facebook.com/nancy.greene.595335

Nancy D. Greene is the CEO at N D Greene PC where she loves working with other women and helping them avoid legal landmines while navigate the very stormy waters of running a business in today's litigious society. Repeatedly introduced as "not your typical lawyer," Nancy demystifies legal "mumbo-jumbo."

With 30 of legal experience, Nancy has been a national speaker since 2014. She published *Navigating Legal Landmines* an Amazon Best Seller in 2017. She specializes in advising businesses about employment law, employee dishonesty issues, business law, mergers and acquisitions, shareholder agreements and disputes, ongoing operations, and bankruptcy.

In *Speak Your Way to Sales*, Nancy shares how to speak about tough issues on the stage and in your business.

Beyond the law, Nancy writes fiction and historical romance, enjoys riding and all things beach related. She lives on a horse farm with her husband and far too many animals (according to him).

Education, Certifications, & Accreditations

Juris Doctorate, Catholic University, Washington DC, 1995
Bar Associations, Virginia (1995); Maryland (1996), DC (1996)
Publisher/writer, *Navigating Legal Landmines, 2017*
YouTube Channel, www.youtube.com/@attorneynancygreene8669
Founder, N D Greene PC, January 2019

Find out how to navigate Legal Landmines

Scan the QR Code to:

- ☑ Schedule a consultation
- ☑ Book Nancy as a speaker
- ☑ Watch videos explaining legal issues
- ☑ Find answers to legal questions

Chapter 3: The Encore Effect: Systems That Keep the Conversation Going by Tracy Walker

Tracy Walker

TW Creative Design

www.twreativedesign.com

 @twcreativedesign

@tracy-walker-twcd

Tracy Walker is the tech-savvy, systems-loving strategist behind TW Creative Design! As an entrepreneur, speaker, and digital powerhouse, Tracy helps creative business owners ditch the overwhelm and build websites and systems that work for you. With over 32 years of customer service know-how and a knack for streamlining chaos, she turns "tech tangles" into smooth, scalable solutions.

Whether you're stuck in content creation overload or knee-deep in launch stress, Tracy's your go-to guide for clarity, structure, and sustainable growth. When she's not organizing digital empires, you'll find her empowering entrepreneurs to stop duct-taping their business together and start thriving with smart strategy.

Education, Certifications, & Accreditations

- BS from Iowa State University
- Website Development & Design Certification from Des Moines Area Community College
- Emotional Intelligence Graduate from Boston Breakthrough Academy
- Leadership Training from Boston Breakthrough Academy
- Go High Level Technical Training (Admin Certification in progress)
- Marketing Certification through The Gold Digger Girl

Ready to Turn Applause into Clients?

Discover the Secret System Top Speakers Use to Keep the Conversation Going

Scan the QR Code to access:

☑ Capture leads live during your talks (with QR or text-to-opt-in tools)
☑ Build automated follow-ups that book clients while you're offstage
☑ Design a website + funnel that work 24/7
☑ Create systems that turn every event into ongoing revenue

Ready to Keep the Encore Alive?

Download your free copy of **The Speaker's Encore Workbook** and start turning your talks into a repeatable, automated client system today.

Molly Ruland
Heartcast Media

heartcastmedia.com

Molly has helmed her multimedia companies for over two decades and is now a trailblazer in the branded podcast production realm. Based in DC but managing her operations from Costa Rica, Molly's expertise spans producing top-ranking podcasts across various genres. Her client roster is impressively diverse, encompassing the Department of Health, DC Government, NATO, dating coaches, and former NBA players, consistently delivering high-quality, strategic, branded content across the board.

Under Molly's leadership, Heartcast Media has become synonymous with premier branded podcast production, aiding businesses in boosting revenue and fostering strategic relationships over the last 6 years. With a deep understanding of podcasting dynamics, content creation, and guest booking, Molly is a sought-after speaker who brings valuable insights to every engagement.

Living next to a volcano in Costa Rica with her three dogs, she embodies the philosophy that "listening is the revolution," driving her global business forward with passion and innovation. Prospect Clip is an extension of the work she has done for years by enabling sales teams of all capabilities and levels.

Scan this to get access to my "always a yes" list of podcasts

Scan the QR Code to access:

☑ 15% off just for reading

Speak Your Way to Sales

www.proposals.heartcastmedia.com/special-offer

Heather McElrath

Sandbox Communications

sandboxcom.ai

linkedin.com/in/hmcelrath/

Heather McElrath is the founder of Sandbox Communications, an AI-powered digital marketing and communications agency that helps businesses and thought leaders get seen, heard, and trusted online.

With more than 20 years of experience in public relations and marketing, Heather has guided national associations, fintech innovators, and Fortune 100 brands in strengthening their messaging, visibility, and credibility. Her work blends human strategy with AI speed—bridging traditional PR, digital marketing, and SEO to help organizations connect with confidence.

In *Speak Your Way to Sales*, Heather shares a practical PR playbook for speakers—showing how to turn one-time engagements into ongoing visibility opportunities.

She also teaches PR Essentials at the Borough of Manhattan Community College, helping the next generation of communicators build confidence and career readiness. Heather lives in Chantilly, Va., and enjoys yoga, champagne, and travel.

<u>Education, Certifications, & Accreditations</u>

- MBA, Marketing, The George Washington University
- B.A., Journalism, Virginia Tech
- Leadership Essentials Certificate, Cornell University

sandboxcom.ai

Turn Your Stage Presence into Media Presence

Scan the QR code to download a free 5-minute speaker pitch template.

Discover how to:

- Land media coverage and podcast interviews
- Build visibility with simple, repeatable systems
- Turn your message into media opportunities that last

SCAN ME

Your voice deserves a bigger audience.
This is where it starts.

Chapter 6: Repurpose to Sell: Turning Every Talk into a Content Engine by Karlyn Ankrom

Karlyn Ankrom

Oh Snap! Social

OhSnapSocial.com

LinkedIn.com/in/karlynankrom

Instagram.com/ohsnapsocialkarlyn

Karlyn Ankrom is the founder of Oh Snap! Social and creator of the Expert Excellence Engine, a strategic content program that helps nonfiction authors turn their books from "expensive business cards" into consistent, engaging content that builds authority and drives results.

With over 20 years of experience in social media strategy and communications, Karlyn has helped hundreds of authors, speakers, and business owners make sense of social media through practical systems, clear storytelling, and strategies that actually stick. Her signature framework helps experts show up online with clarity, confidence, and consistency—without burning out.

In *Speak Your Way to Sales*, Karlyn's chapter, "Repurpose to Sell – Turning Every Talk into a Content Engine," teaches how to turn every podcast interview, keynote, or panel into content that keeps working long after the mic drops.

When she's not deep in the social media trenches, Karlyn is teaching dance, keeping up with her daughter, or sneaking away for iced coffee and breakfast sammies with her husband.

Education, Certifications, & Accreditations

- Instructor for American Marketing Association
- B.A. Journalism, James Madison University

OHSNAPSOCIAL.COM

Turn One Talk Into Twenty Touchpoints

You already poured hours into that keynote.
Why let it stop there?
Download 20 Fresh Ways to Repackage Your
Content Cheat Sheet that helps speakers,
authors, and experts turn one talk into a month
of scroll-stopping posts, reels, and articles.

**KEEP YOUR STAGE MOMENTUM GOING
— LONG AFTER THE LIGHTS DIM.**

Chapter 7: Delegate Like a Speaker: How a Virtual Assistant Expands Your Stage
by Jennifer Crawford

Jennifer Crawford

Co-CEO, Sparent, LLC
Co-CEO, Move Forward
Virtual Assistants, LLC

sparent.co
moveforwardvirtualassistants.com

@sparentco
@moveforwardvas

Jennifer Crawford is the co-founder and co-CEO of two virtual assistant agencies. In 2018, she and business partner Meredith Eaton, co-founded Sparent, where she manages a talent pool of stay-at-home moms who help overwhelmed business owners get things accomplished. In 2022, Jennifer and Meredith bought Move Forward Virtual Assistants which specializes in the administrative support of over 100 mental health practices.

With over 30 years of experience in growing service-based businesses, Jennifer has built multiple seven-figure companies and understands how important delegation and superior support are to any business's success.

In *Speak Your Way to Sales*, Jennifer shares how delegating to a virtual assistant can take you from a great speaker to an in-demand speaking professional.

In addition to running two virtual assistant agencies, Jennifer enjoys spending time in the Blue Ridge Mountains, road trips, reading, hiking, and improv.

Education, Certifications, & Accreditations
- Founded DC PodFest in 2015, the only podcasting conference in the DC Metro Area, and booked speakers nationally.
- Has helped hundreds of business owners and speakers work with virtual assistants to get the most out of their speaking opportunities.

Imagine a speaking strategy that runs even while you're off the clock.

No more missed opportunities.

No more overwhelmed late-night research sessions.

No more feeling like you "should" be doing more to get your message out.

That system is absolutely possible — and you don't have to build it yourself.

Download Your Free Resource:

Delegate Your Way to Speaking Gigs

A practical, done-for-you guide that includes:

- Templates
- Scripts
- Checklists
- And More!

Your voice deserves a bigger platform.

Let a VA help you get there — without burning yourself out.

Mary Sue Dahill

Work Smarter Digital

www.worksmarterdigital.com

@worksmarterdigital

@marysuedahill

Mary Sue Dahill is the founder and CEO of Work Smarter Digital, helping service-based founders streamline operations, integrate AI, and scale profitably with smart CRM systems and automation. With more than 25 years in technology, startups, and business management, she has guided hundreds of entrepreneurs in building sales systems that turn chaos into consistent, scalable revenue. She is a HighLevel Certified Admin and the author of The Boutique Effect and The Solopreneur's Dilemma.

In *Speak Your Way to Sales*, Mary Sue led the book's development and contributes a chapter on how speakers can stop chasing gigs and start booking them with confidence using her Revenue Accelerator for Speakers—a practical system for organizing outreach, tracking opportunities, and landing more paid and referral-driving engagements.

Outside of work, Mary Sue enjoys slow mornings with her husband and two mini dachshunds, sipping coffee on the patio, and planning travel adventures from her home in Arlington, Virginia.

Education, Certifications, & Accreditations

- Master of Science in Management of Information Technology, University of Virginia
- Certified HighLevel Admin, HighLevel (2024)

This Is Exactly How You Get More Booked Gigs!

Scan the QR Code to access:

☑ Your free Speaker's Booking Pipeline Toolkit

☑ Special offers for the Revenue Accelerator for Speakers

Stop chasing gigs. Start booking them—with confidence, consistency, and a system that works.

Katie Nelson

Sales UpRising

salesuprising.com

linkedin.com/company/salesuprising

facebook.com/salesuprising

Katie Nelson is a business strategist at Sales UpRising, where she empowers solopreneurs with the tools and strategies to break into six-figure revenues.

With 30+ years of experience in sales, Katie has helped 200+ entrepreneurs, helped generate $7.59 million in revenue, and built 3 businesses. She specializes in business coaching and is an expert in sales.

In Speak Your Way To Sales, Katie shares actionable tips to help you turn speaking gigs into growth for your business.

Beyond business consulting, Katie enjoys keeping life creative with painting, doodling, reading, and connecting with people from all walks of life. She lives in Northern Virginia with her husband, Adam, and spicy fur baby, Julius.

<u>Education, Certifications, & Accreditations</u>

- Bachelor's of Interdisciplinary Studies, Communications & Sociology, ASU 2001
- Smart CEO, Brava Award Winner, 2015
- Washington Business Journal, Best Places to Work, 2015
- Start Up Certified
- 3x Biz Owner

YOU'RE INVITED: STRAIGHT UP!

All Integrity. All Accountability. All the Time.

This is not a networking group. This is not a "learning more" club. This is an opportunity to say YES to you! It is an accountability group designed to help you stay accountable to your Speak Your Way to Sales goals.

This group will help you stay accountable to your GOALS: how many stages you book, staying on track with follow up, your pitching from stage, how much you earn from stages (front end and back end)!

Everything that has to do with Speak Your Way to Sales is how this group can support you!

Join now and get a FREE month of Straight UP!